Marketing Strategy And Executi
Complete Self-Assessment Guid

The guidance in this Self-Assessment is b_____ __ _____ _____ And Execution best practices and standards in business process architecture, design and quality management. The guidance is also based on the professional judgment of the individual collaborators listed in the Acknowledgments.

Notice of rights

Trademarks

Table of Contents

About The Art of Service

The Art of Service, Business Process Architects since 2000, is dedicated to helping stakeholders achieve excellence.

Defining, designing, creating, and implementing a process to solve a stakeholders challenge or meet an objective is the most valuable role… In EVERY group, company, organization and department.

Unless you're talking a one-time, single-use project, there should be a process. Whether that process is managed and implemented by humans, AI, or a combination of the two, it needs to be designed by someone with a complex enough perspective to ask the right questions.

Someone capable of asking the right questions and step back and say, 'What are we really trying to accomplish here? And is there a different way to look at it?'

With The Art of Service's Standard Requirements Self-Assessments, we empower people who can do just that — whether their title is marketer, entrepreneur, manager, salesperson, consultant, Business Process Manager, executive assistant, IT Manager, CIO etc... —they are the people who rule the future. They are people who watch the process as it happens, and ask the right questions to make the process work better.

Contact us when you need any support with this Self-Assessment and any help with templates, blue-prints and examples of standard documents you might need:

http://theartofservice.com
service@theartofservice.com

Included Resources - how to access

Included with your purchase of the book is the Marketing

Strategy And Execution Self-Assessment Spreadsheet Dashboard which contains all questions and Self-Assessment areas and auto-generates insights, graphs, and project RACI planning - all with examples to get you started right away.

How? Simply send an email to
access@theartofservice.com
with this books' title in the subject to get the Marketing Strategy And Execution Self Assessment Tool right away.

You will receive the following contents with New and Updated specific criteria:

- The latest quick edition of the book in PDF

- The latest complete edition of the book in PDF, which criteria correspond to the criteria in...

- The Self-Assessment Excel Dashboard, and...

- Example pre-filled Self-Assessment Excel Dashboard to get familiar with results generation

- In-depth specific Checklists covering the topic

- Project management checklists and templates to assist with implementation

INCLUDES LIFETIME SELF ASSESSMENT UPDATES

Every self assessment comes with Lifetime Updates and Lifetime Free Updated Books. Lifetime Updates is an industry-first feature which allows you to receive verified self assessment updates, ensuring you always have the most accurate information at your fingertips.

Get it now- you will be glad you did - do it now, before you forget.

Send an email to **access@theartofservice.com** with this books' title in the subject to get the Marketing Strategy And Execution Self Assessment Tool right away.

Purpose of this Self-Assessment

This Self-Assessment has been developed to improve understanding of the requirements and elements of Marketing Strategy And Execution, based on best practices and standards in business process architecture, design and quality management.

It is designed to allow for a rapid Self-Assessment to determine how closely existing management practices and procedures correspond to the elements of the Self-Assessment.

The criteria of requirements and elements of Marketing Strategy And Execution have been rephrased in the format of a Self-Assessment questionnaire, with a seven-criterion scoring system, as explained in this document.

In this format, even with limited background knowledge of Marketing Strategy And Execution, a manager can quickly review existing operations to determine how they measure up to the standards. This in turn can serve as the starting point of a 'gap analysis' to identify management tools or system elements that might usefully be implemented in the organization to help improve overall performance.

How to use the Self-Assessment

On the following pages are a series of questions to identify to what extent your Marketing Strategy And Execution initiative is complete in comparison to the requirements set in standards.

To facilitate answering the questions, there is a space in front of each question to enter a score on a scale of '1' to '5'.

1 Strongly Disagree

2 Disagree

3 Neutral

4 Agree

5 Strongly Agree

Read the question and rate it with the following in front of mind:

**'In my belief,
the answer to this question is clearly defined'.**

There are two ways in which you can choose to interpret this statement;
   1. how aware are you that the answer to the question is clearly defined
   2. for more in-depth analysis you can choose to gather evidence and confirm the answer to the question. This obviously will take more time, most Self-Assessment users opt for the first way to interpret the question and dig deeper later on based on the outcome of the overall Self-Assessment.

A score of '1' would mean that the answer is not clear at all, where a '5' would mean the answer is crystal clear and defined. Leave emtpy when the question is not applicable or you don't want to answer it, you can skip it without affecting your score. Write your score in the space provided.

After you have responded to all the appropriate statements in each section, compute your average score for that section, using the formula provided, and round to the nearest tenth. Then transfer to the corresponding spoke in the Marketing Strategy And Execution Scorecard on the second next page of the Self-Assessment.

Your completed Marketing Strategy And Execution Scorecard will give you a clear presentation of which Marketing Strategy And Execution areas need attention.

Marketing Strategy And Execution Scorecard Example

Example of how the finalized Scorecard can look like:

Marketing Strategy And Execution Scorecard

Your Scores:

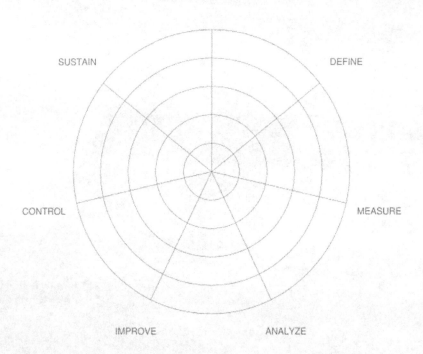

BEGINNING OF THE SELF-ASSESSMENT:

CRITERION #1: RECOGNIZE

INTENT: Be aware of the need for change. Recognize that there is an unfavorable variation, problem or symptom.

In my belief, the answer to this question is clearly defined:

5 Strongly Agree

4 Agree

3 Neutral

2 Disagree

1 Strongly Disagree

1. Does Marketing Strategy and Execution create potential expectations in other areas that need to be recognized and considered?
<--- Score

2. What training and capacity building actions are needed to implement proposed reforms?
<--- Score

3. How do you take a forward-looking perspective in identifying Marketing Strategy and Execution research related to market response and models?
<--- Score

4. What are the stakeholder objectives to be achieved with Marketing Strategy and Execution?
<--- Score

5. What Marketing Strategy and Execution capabilities do you need?
<--- Score

6. What Marketing Strategy and Execution problem should be solved?
<--- Score

7. What resources or support might you need?
<--- Score

8. When a Marketing Strategy and Execution manager recognizes a problem, what options are available?
<--- Score

9. As a sponsor, customer or management, how important is it to meet goals, objectives?
<--- Score

10. Who needs to know?
<--- Score

11. How can auditing be a preventative security measure?
<--- Score

12. Does your organization need more Marketing Strategy and Execution education?
<--- Score

13. What are the expected benefits of Marketing Strategy and Execution to the stakeholder?
<--- Score

14. What situation(s) led to this Marketing Strategy and Execution Self Assessment?
<--- Score

15. Who else hopes to benefit from it?
<--- Score

16. What would happen if Marketing Strategy and Execution weren't done?
<--- Score

17. What activities does the governance board need to consider?
<--- Score

18. Are there any revenue recognition issues?
<--- Score

19. What are the clients issues and concerns?
<--- Score

20. Which needs are not included or involved?
<--- Score

21. Who should resolve the Marketing Strategy and Execution issues?
<--- Score

22. Who needs to know about Marketing Strategy and Execution?

<--- Score

23. Are problem definition and motivation clearly presented?

<--- Score

24. Which issues are too important to ignore?

<--- Score

25. How many trainings, in total, are needed?

<--- Score

26. What are the timeframes required to resolve each of the issues/problems?

<--- Score

27. What are your needs in relation to Marketing Strategy and Execution skills, labor, equipment, and markets?

<--- Score

28. Would you recognize a threat from the inside?

<--- Score

29. Will a response program recognize when a crisis occurs and provide some level of response?

<--- Score

30. Will it solve real problems?

<--- Score

31. Are employees recognized for desired behaviors?

<--- Score

32. Looking at each person individually – does every one have the qualities which are needed to work in this group?
<--- Score

33. How are the Marketing Strategy and Execution's objectives aligned to the group's overall stakeholder strategy?
<--- Score

34. How are you going to measure success?
<--- Score

35. How do you identify the kinds of information that you will need?
<--- Score

36. What Marketing Strategy and Execution events should you attend?
<--- Score

37. How do you recognize an objection?
<--- Score

38. What creative shifts do you need to take?
<--- Score

39. Is the need for organizational change recognized?
<--- Score

40. Can management personnel recognize the monetary benefit of Marketing Strategy and Execution?
<--- Score

41. What is the recognized need?

<--- Score

42. Who defines the rules in relation to any given issue?
<--- Score

43. Is it clear when you think of the day ahead of you what activities and tasks you need to complete?
<--- Score

44. Are employees recognized or rewarded for performance that demonstrates the highest levels of integrity?
<--- Score

45. Why is this needed?
<--- Score

46. What does Marketing Strategy and Execution success mean to the stakeholders?
<--- Score

47. Will Marketing Strategy and Execution deliverables need to be tested and, if so, by whom?
<--- Score

48. What is the Marketing Strategy and Execution problem definition? What do you need to resolve?
<--- Score

49. Whom do you really need or want to serve?
<--- Score

50. What is the extent or complexity of the Marketing Strategy and Execution problem?

<--- Score

51. Are controls defined to recognize and contain problems?
<--- Score

52. Do you have/need 24-hour access to key personnel?
<--- Score

53. To what extent does each concerned units management team recognize Marketing Strategy and Execution as an effective investment?
<--- Score

54. What problems are you facing and how do you consider Marketing Strategy and Execution will circumvent those obstacles?
<--- Score

55. What is the problem or issue?
<--- Score

56. Who needs what information?
<--- Score

57. Are your goals realistic? Do you need to redefine your problem? Perhaps the problem has changed or maybe you have reached your goal and need to set a new one?
<--- Score

58. How does it fit into your organizational needs and tasks?
<--- Score

59. How are training requirements identified?
<--- Score

60. Do you need to avoid or amend any Marketing Strategy and Execution activities?
<--- Score

61. Is the quality assurance team identified?
<--- Score

62. What is the smallest subset of the problem you can usefully solve?
<--- Score

63. Are there any specific expectations or concerns about the Marketing Strategy and Execution team, Marketing Strategy and Execution itself?
<--- Score

64. To what extent would your organization benefit from being recognized as a award recipient?
<--- Score

65. How do you assess your Marketing Strategy and Execution workforce capability and capacity needs, including skills, competencies, and staffing levels?
<--- Score

66. Where do you need to exercise leadership?
<--- Score

67. Are there Marketing Strategy and Execution problems defined?
<--- Score

68. What tools and technologies are needed for a

custom Marketing Strategy and Execution project?
<--- Score

69. Do you need different information or graphics?
<--- Score

70. What should be considered when identifying available resources, constraints, and deadlines?
<--- Score

71. What else needs to be measured?
<--- Score

72. Do you know what you need to know about Marketing Strategy and Execution?
<--- Score

73. How do you recognize an Marketing Strategy and Execution objection?
<--- Score

74. What is the problem and/or vulnerability?
<--- Score

75. What needs to be done?
<--- Score

76. Are there recognized Marketing Strategy and Execution problems?
<--- Score

77. What prevents you from making the changes you know will make you a more effective Marketing Strategy and Execution leader?
<--- Score

78. Are there regulatory / compliance issues?
<--- Score

79. Do you recognize Marketing Strategy and Execution achievements?
<--- Score

80. What are the Marketing Strategy and Execution resources needed?
<--- Score

81. Are you dealing with any of the same issues today as yesterday? What can you do about this?
<--- Score

82. Is it needed?
<--- Score

83. Which information does the Marketing Strategy and Execution business case need to include?
<--- Score

84. Consider your own Marketing Strategy and Execution project, what types of organizational problems do you think might be causing or affecting your problem, based on the work done so far?
<--- Score

85. What do employees need in the short term?
<--- Score

86. Who needs budgets?
<--- Score

87. How much are sponsors, customers, partners, stakeholders involved in Marketing Strategy and Execution? In other words, what are the risks, if Marketing Strategy and Execution does not deliver successfully?
<--- Score

88. What information do users need?
<--- Score

89. What are the minority interests and what amount of minority interests can be recognized?
<--- Score

90. Who are your key stakeholders who need to sign off?
<--- Score

91. What Marketing Strategy and Execution coordination do you need?
<--- Score

92. Have you identified your Marketing Strategy and Execution key performance indicators?
<--- Score

93. Will new equipment/products be required to facilitate Marketing Strategy and Execution delivery, for example is new software needed?
<--- Score

94. Did you miss any major Marketing Strategy and Execution issues?
<--- Score

95. What needs to stay?

<--- Score

96. Where is training needed?
<--- Score

97. Why the need?
<--- Score

Add up total points for this section:
_ _ _ _ _ = Total points for this section

Divided by: _ _ _ _ _ _ (number of
statements answered) = _ _ _ _ _ _
Average score for this section

Transfer your score to the Marketing
Strategy and Execution Index at the
beginning of the Self-Assessment.

CRITERION #2: DEFINE:

INTENT: Formulate the stakeholder problem. Define the problem, needs and objectives.

In my belief, the answer to this question is clearly defined:

5 Strongly Agree

4 Agree

3 Neutral

2 Disagree

1 Strongly Disagree

1. Is there a completed SIPOC representation, describing the Suppliers, Inputs, Process, Outputs, and Customers?
<--- Score

2. What Marketing Strategy and Execution services do you require?
<--- Score

3. Are there different segments of customers?
<--- Score

4. Have all of the relationships been defined properly?
<--- Score

5. What was the context?
<--- Score

6. What are the dynamics of the communication plan?
<--- Score

7. Is the work to date meeting requirements?
<--- Score

8. How do you keep key subject matter experts in the loop?
<--- Score

9. Has a project plan, Gantt chart, or similar been developed/completed?
<--- Score

10. Is there a Marketing Strategy and Execution management charter, including stakeholder case, problem and goal statements, scope, milestones, roles and responsibilities, communication plan?
<--- Score

11. Is the current 'as is' process being followed? If not, what are the discrepancies?
<--- Score

12. What happens if Marketing Strategy and Execution's scope changes?
<--- Score

13. What is the definition of Marketing Strategy and Execution excellence?
<--- Score

14. What is in scope?
<--- Score

15. Are improvement team members fully trained on Marketing Strategy and Execution?
<--- Score

16. Who are the Marketing Strategy and Execution improvement team members, including Management Leads and Coaches?
<--- Score

17. What critical content must be communicated – who, what, when, where, and how?
<--- Score

18. What defines best in class?
<--- Score

19. Is there a completed, verified, and validated high-level 'as is' (not 'should be' or 'could be') stakeholder process map?
<--- Score

20. What are the Marketing Strategy and Execution tasks and definitions?
<--- Score

21. Has the Marketing Strategy and Execution work been fairly and/or equitably divided and delegated among team members who are qualified and capable

to perform the work? Has everyone contributed?
<--- Score

22. What baselines are required to be defined and managed?
<--- Score

23. What is a worst-case scenario for losses?
<--- Score

24. Is data collected and displayed to better understand customer(s) critical needs and requirements.
<--- Score

25. Do you have organizational privacy requirements?
<--- Score

26. Has the direction changed at all during the course of Marketing Strategy and Execution? If so, when did it change and why?
<--- Score

27. Is the team equipped with available and reliable resources?
<--- Score

28. What are the Roles and Responsibilities for each team member and its leadership? Where is this documented?
<--- Score

29. Has everyone on the team, including the team leaders, been properly trained?
<--- Score

30. Is Marketing Strategy and Execution linked to key stakeholder goals and objectives?
<--- Score

31. How was the 'as is' process map developed, reviewed, verified and validated?
<--- Score

32. When is the estimated completion date?
<--- Score

33. Has/have the customer(s) been identified?
<--- Score

34. How do you gather Marketing Strategy and Execution requirements?
<--- Score

35. What sources do you use to gather information for a Marketing Strategy and Execution study?
<--- Score

36. How will the Marketing Strategy and Execution team and the group measure complete success of Marketing Strategy and Execution?
<--- Score

37. Have the customer needs been translated into specific, measurable requirements? How?
<--- Score

38. What are the rough order estimates on cost savings/opportunities that Marketing Strategy and Execution brings?
<--- Score

39. Is the team formed and are team leaders (Coaches and Management Leads) assigned?
<--- Score

40. What is the definition of success?
<--- Score

41. Is the scope of Marketing Strategy and Execution defined?
<--- Score

42. Does the scope remain the same?
<--- Score

43. The political context: who holds power?
<--- Score

44. How do you manage scope?
<--- Score

45. Are task requirements clearly defined?
<--- Score

46. Is it clearly defined in and to your organization what you do?
<--- Score

47. Have specific policy objectives been defined?
<--- Score

48. Who defines (or who defined) the rules and roles?
<--- Score

49. Are there any constraints known that bear on the

ability to perform Marketing Strategy and Execution work? How is the team addressing them?
<--- Score

50. When is/was the Marketing Strategy and Execution start date?
<--- Score

51. Is the team adequately staffed with the desired cross-functionality? If not, what additional resources are available to the team?
<--- Score

52. How are consistent Marketing Strategy and Execution definitions important?
<--- Score

53. Has a high-level 'as is' process map been completed, verified and validated?
<--- Score

54. How do you think the partners involved in Marketing Strategy and Execution would have defined success?
<--- Score

55. How do you manage unclear Marketing Strategy and Execution requirements?
<--- Score

56. What is out-of-scope initially?
<--- Score

57. When are meeting minutes sent out? Who is on the distribution list?
<--- Score

58. Are the Marketing Strategy and Execution requirements complete?

<--- Score

59. Have all basic functions of Marketing Strategy and Execution been defined?

<--- Score

60. Are audit criteria, scope, frequency and methods defined?

<--- Score

61. Are roles and responsibilities formally defined?

<--- Score

62. What are (control) requirements for Marketing Strategy and Execution Information?

<--- Score

63. Has a team charter been developed and communicated?

<--- Score

64. What are the tasks and definitions?

<--- Score

65. Is the improvement team aware of the different versions of a process: what they think it is vs. what it actually is vs. what it should be vs. what it could be?

<--- Score

66. Is Marketing Strategy and Execution required?

<--- Score

67. Has anyone else (internal or external to the group)

attempted to solve this problem or a similar one before? If so, what knowledge can be leveraged from these previous efforts?
<--- Score

68. Who is gathering information?
<--- Score

69. What Marketing Strategy and Execution requirements should be gathered?
<--- Score

70. Do the problem and goal statements meet the SMART criteria (specific, measurable, attainable, relevant, and time-bound)?
<--- Score

71. What sort of initial information to gather?
<--- Score

72. Do you have a Marketing Strategy and Execution success story or case study ready to tell and share?
<--- Score

73. How will variation in the actual durations of each activity be dealt with to ensure that the expected Marketing Strategy and Execution results are met?
<--- Score

74. Is the Marketing Strategy and Execution scope complete and appropriately sized?
<--- Score

75. Are resources adequate for the scope?
<--- Score

76. Is full participation by members in regularly held team meetings guaranteed?
<--- Score

77. How do you manage changes in Marketing Strategy and Execution requirements?
<--- Score

78. How and when will the baselines be defined?
<--- Score

79. Is scope creep really all bad news?
<--- Score

80. Is the Marketing Strategy and Execution scope manageable?
<--- Score

81. What key stakeholder process output measure(s) does Marketing Strategy and Execution leverage and how?
<--- Score

82. What scope do you want your strategy to cover?
<--- Score

83. How do you gather the stories?
<--- Score

84. Does the team have regular meetings?
<--- Score

85. Is there any additional Marketing Strategy and Execution definition of success?
<--- Score

86. Will team members perform Marketing Strategy and Execution work when assigned and in a timely fashion?
<--- Score

87. What are the Marketing Strategy and Execution use cases?
<--- Score

88. What specifically is the problem? Where does it occur? When does it occur? What is its extent?
<--- Score

89. What constraints exist that might impact the team?
<--- Score

90. What is the worst case scenario?
<--- Score

91. Are the Marketing Strategy and Execution requirements testable?
<--- Score

92. What information do you gather?
<--- Score

93. How do you build the right business case?
<--- Score

94. Are accountability and ownership for Marketing Strategy and Execution clearly defined?
<--- Score

95. How do you hand over Marketing Strategy and

Execution context?
<--- Score

96. How does the Marketing Strategy and Execution manager ensure against scope creep?
<--- Score

97. How do you catch Marketing Strategy and Execution definition inconsistencies?
<--- Score

98. Are customer(s) identified and segmented according to their different needs and requirements?
<--- Score

99. What is the scope of the Marketing Strategy and Execution effort?
<--- Score

100. How have you defined all Marketing Strategy and Execution requirements first?
<--- Score

101. What is the context?
<--- Score

102. How is the team tracking and documenting its work?
<--- Score

103. What customer feedback methods were used to solicit their input?
<--- Score

104. What is in the scope and what is not in scope?
<--- Score

105. What gets examined?
<--- Score

106. How often are the team meetings?
<--- Score

107. Are approval levels defined for contracts and supplements to contracts?
<--- Score

108. What knowledge or experience is required?
<--- Score

109. Who approved the Marketing Strategy and Execution scope?
<--- Score

110. Has the improvement team collected the 'voice of the customer' (obtained feedback – qualitative and quantitative)?
<--- Score

111. What are the core elements of the Marketing Strategy and Execution business case?
<--- Score

112. Has your scope been defined?
<--- Score

113. What intelligence can you gather?
<--- Score

114. What system do you use for gathering Marketing Strategy and Execution information?
<--- Score

115. What information should you gather?
<--- Score

116. Is there regularly 100% attendance at the team meetings? If not, have appointed substitutes attended to preserve cross-functionality and full representation?
<--- Score

117. How do you gather requirements?
<--- Score

118. How can the value of Marketing Strategy and Execution be defined?
<--- Score

119. Will team members regularly document their Marketing Strategy and Execution work?
<--- Score

120. If substitutes have been appointed, have they been briefed on the Marketing Strategy and Execution goals and received regular communications as to the progress to date?
<--- Score

121. What are the record-keeping requirements of Marketing Strategy and Execution activities?
<--- Score

122. What are the compelling stakeholder reasons for embarking on Marketing Strategy and Execution?
<--- Score

123. Has a Marketing Strategy and Execution

requirement not been met?
<--- Score

124. What is the scope?
<--- Score

125. Why are you doing Marketing Strategy and Execution and what is the scope?
<--- Score

126. Are required metrics defined, what are they?
<--- Score

127. Is special Marketing Strategy and Execution user knowledge required?
<--- Score

128. What would be the goal or target for a Marketing Strategy and Execution's improvement team?
<--- Score

129. How would you define Marketing Strategy and Execution leadership?
<--- Score

130. What is the scope of the Marketing Strategy and Execution work?
<--- Score

131. Who is gathering Marketing Strategy and Execution information?
<--- Score

132. Are all requirements met?
<--- Score

133. Do you all define Marketing Strategy and Execution in the same way?
<--- Score

134. What scope to assess?
<--- Score

135. How did the Marketing Strategy and Execution manager receive input to the development of a Marketing Strategy and Execution improvement plan and the estimated completion dates/times of each activity?
<--- Score

136. Is there a critical path to deliver Marketing Strategy and Execution results?
<--- Score

137. Are different versions of process maps needed to account for the different types of inputs?
<--- Score

138. What are the boundaries of the scope? What is in bounds and what is not? What is the start point? What is the stop point?
<--- Score

139. How would you define the culture at your organization, how susceptible is it to Marketing Strategy and Execution changes?
<--- Score

140. Is Marketing Strategy and Execution currently on schedule according to the plan?
<--- Score

Add up total points for this section:
_____ = Total points for this section

Divided by: _____ (number of
statements answered) = _____
Average score for this section

Transfer your score to the Marketing
Strategy and Execution Index at the
beginning of the Self-Assessment.

CRITERION #3: MEASURE:

INTENT: Gather the correct data. Measure the current performance and evolution of the situation.

In my belief, the answer to this question is clearly defined:

5 Strongly Agree

4 Agree

3 Neutral

2 Disagree

1 Strongly Disagree

1. What is the cause of any Marketing Strategy and Execution gaps?
<--- Score

2. How do you verify Marketing Strategy and Execution completeness and accuracy?
<--- Score

3. What does a Test Case verify?

<--- Score

4. Why do the measurements/indicators matter?
<--- Score

5. Are you taking your company in the direction of better and revenue or cheaper and cost?
<--- Score

6. How frequently do you track Marketing Strategy and Execution measures?
<--- Score

7. What is an unallowable cost?
<--- Score

8. Have you included everything in your Marketing Strategy and Execution cost models?
<--- Score

9. Does management have the right priorities among projects?
<--- Score

10. Who pays the cost?
<--- Score

11. What does your operating model cost?
<--- Score

12. What evidence is there and what is measured?
<--- Score

13. What do people want to verify?
<--- Score

14. Which costs should be taken into account?
<--- Score

15. How is progress measured?
<--- Score

16. How is performance measured?
<--- Score

17. What are the uncertainties surrounding estimates of impact?
<--- Score

18. What users will be impacted?
<--- Score

19. What measurements are being captured?
<--- Score

20. What are allowable costs?
<--- Score

21. What happens if cost savings do not materialize?
<--- Score

22. How much does it cost?
<--- Score

23. What are the costs of delaying Marketing Strategy and Execution action?
<--- Score

24. What would it cost to replace your technology?
<--- Score

25. What causes mismanagement?

<--- Score

26. When should you bother with diagrams?
<--- Score

27. What do you measure and why?
<--- Score

28. What are hidden Marketing Strategy and Execution quality costs?
<--- Score

29. Is the solution cost-effective?
<--- Score

30. What are your primary costs, revenues, assets?
<--- Score

31. Is a follow-up focused external Marketing Strategy and Execution review required?
<--- Score

32. Are there any easy-to-implement alternatives to Marketing Strategy and Execution? Sometimes other solutions are available that do not require the cost implications of a full-blown project?
<--- Score

33. Why a Marketing Strategy and Execution focus?
<--- Score

34. Are there competing Marketing Strategy and Execution priorities?
<--- Score

35. Are the Marketing Strategy and Execution benefits

worth its costs?

<--- Score

36. Do you have any cost Marketing Strategy and Execution limitation requirements?

<--- Score

37. How do you control the overall costs of your work processes?

<--- Score

38. Are missed Marketing Strategy and Execution opportunities costing your organization money?

<--- Score

39. How will you measure success?

<--- Score

40. How do you measure efficient delivery of Marketing Strategy and Execution services?

<--- Score

41. How will costs be allocated?

<--- Score

42. How long to keep data and how to manage retention costs?

<--- Score

43. How can you measure the performance?

<--- Score

44. How do you verify the Marketing Strategy and Execution requirements quality?

<--- Score

45. How are costs allocated?
<--- Score

46. How will your organization measure success?
<--- Score

47. What are the current costs of the Marketing Strategy and Execution process?
<--- Score

48. How do you aggregate measures across priorities?
<--- Score

49. How do you stay flexible and focused to recognize larger Marketing Strategy and Execution results?
<--- Score

50. Who is involved in verifying compliance?
<--- Score

51. How will measures be used to manage and adapt?
<--- Score

52. Is it possible to estimate the impact of unanticipated complexity such as wrong or failed assumptions, feedback, etcetera on proposed reforms?
<--- Score

53. Are you able to realize any cost savings?
<--- Score

54. Which measures and indicators matter?
<--- Score

55. What is the Marketing Strategy and Execution business impact?

<--- Score

56. What are the costs?

<--- Score

57. How do you measure success?

<--- Score

58. What are the Marketing Strategy and Execution investment costs?

<--- Score

59. Where can you go to verify the info?

<--- Score

60. What is the cost of rework?

<--- Score

61. How do you measure variability?

<--- Score

62. What could cause you to change course?

<--- Score

63. What does verifying compliance entail?

<--- Score

64. The approach of traditional Marketing Strategy and Execution works for detail complexity but is focused on a systematic approach rather than an understanding of the nature of systems themselves, what approach will permit your organization to deal with the kind of unpredictable emergent behaviors

that dynamic complexity can introduce?

<--- Score

65. What potential environmental factors impact the Marketing Strategy and Execution effort?

<--- Score

66. How to cause the change?

<--- Score

67. What is measured? Why?

<--- Score

68. Are indirect costs charged to the Marketing Strategy and Execution program?

<--- Score

69. What causes investor action?

<--- Score

70. What drives O&M cost?

<--- Score

71. Is the cost worth the Marketing Strategy and Execution effort ?

<--- Score

72. How are you verifying it?

<--- Score

73. How will the Marketing Strategy and Execution data be analyzed?

<--- Score

74. Have you made assumptions about the shape of the future, particularly its impact on your customers

and competitors?

<--- Score

75. What are the types and number of measures to use?

<--- Score

76. How do you verify and develop ideas and innovations?

<--- Score

77. What are the operational costs after Marketing Strategy and Execution deployment?

<--- Score

78. How do you prevent mis-estimating cost?

<--- Score

79. What could cause delays in the schedule?

<--- Score

80. How sensitive must the Marketing Strategy and Execution strategy be to cost?

<--- Score

81. How do you focus on what is right -not who is right?

<--- Score

82. How do you verify performance?

<--- Score

83. How do your measurements capture actionable Marketing Strategy and Execution information for use in exceeding your customers expectations and securing your customers engagement?

<--- Score

84. How is the value delivered by Marketing Strategy and Execution being measured?
<--- Score

85. Where is it measured?
<--- Score

86. What would be a real cause for concern?
<--- Score

87. What causes extra work or rework?
<--- Score

88. Will Marketing Strategy and Execution have an impact on current business continuity, disaster recovery processes and/or infrastructure?
<--- Score

89. What are your customers expectations and measures?
<--- Score

90. Do you have an issue in getting priority?
<--- Score

91. How can you reduce costs?
<--- Score

92. What are the Marketing Strategy and Execution key cost drivers?
<--- Score

93. Have design-to-cost goals been established?
<--- Score

94. How will effects be measured?
<--- Score

95. Are the units of measure consistent?
<--- Score

96. What is the total cost related to deploying
Marketing Strategy and Execution, including any
consulting or professional services?
<--- Score

**97. What are the estimated costs of proposed
changes?**
<--- Score

98. Does the Marketing Strategy and Execution task fit
the client's priorities?
<--- Score

99. How can you reduce the costs of obtaining inputs?
<--- Score

100. How can a Marketing Strategy and Execution test
verify your ideas or assumptions?
<--- Score

101. How will success or failure be measured?
<--- Score

102. What are you verifying?
<--- Score

103. Do the benefits outweigh the costs?
<--- Score

104. Was a business case (cost/benefit) developed?
<--- Score

105. What can be used to verify compliance?
<--- Score

106. Which Marketing Strategy and Execution impacts are significant?
<--- Score

107. How do you measure lifecycle phases?
<--- Score

108. What measurements are possible, practicable and meaningful?
<--- Score

109. What does losing customers cost your organization?
<--- Score

110. What is the total fixed cost?
<--- Score

111. Do you aggressively reward and promote the people who have the biggest impact on creating excellent Marketing Strategy and Execution services/products?
<--- Score

112. Are Marketing Strategy and Execution vulnerabilities categorized and prioritized?
<--- Score

113. How do you verify your resources?
<--- Score

114. How do you verify and validate the Marketing Strategy and Execution data?
<--- Score

115. What are the costs of reform?
<--- Score

116. Are actual costs in line with budgeted costs?
<--- Score

117. What tests verify requirements?
<--- Score

118. What causes innovation to fail or succeed in your organization?
<--- Score

119. Are you aware of what could cause a problem?
<--- Score

120. How can you measure Marketing Strategy and Execution in a systematic way?
<--- Score

121. Is there an opportunity to verify requirements?
<--- Score

122. What is your decision requirements diagram?
<--- Score

123. What is the root cause(s) of the problem?
<--- Score

124. What are your key Marketing Strategy and

Execution organizational performance measures, including key short and longer-term financial measures?
<--- Score

125. Do you verify that corrective actions were taken?
<--- Score

126. Are the measurements objective?
<--- Score

127. Where is the cost?
<--- Score

128. At what cost?
<--- Score

129. How do you verify the authenticity of the data and information used?
<--- Score

130. What relevant entities could be measured?
<--- Score

131. Do you have a flow diagram of what happens?
<--- Score

132. What harm might be caused?
<--- Score

133. How will you measure your Marketing Strategy and Execution effectiveness?
<--- Score

134. Do you effectively measure and reward individual and team performance?

<--- Score

135. When are costs are incurred?
<--- Score

136. What details are required of the Marketing Strategy and Execution cost structure?
<--- Score

137. Are supply costs steady or fluctuating?
<--- Score

138. Did you tackle the cause or the symptom?
<--- Score

139. Are there measurements based on task performance?
<--- Score

140. What are your operating costs?
<--- Score

141. How do you verify if Marketing Strategy and Execution is built right?
<--- Score

Add up total points for this section:
_ _ _ _ _ = Total points for this section

Divided by: _ _ _ _ _ _ (number of statements answered) = _ _ _ _ _ _
Average score for this section

Transfer your score to the Marketing Strategy and Execution Index at the beginning of the Self-Assessment.

CRITERION #4: ANALYZE:

INTENT: Analyze causes, assumptions and hypotheses.

In my belief, the answer to this question is clearly defined:

5 Strongly Agree

4 Agree

3 Neutral

2 Disagree

1 Strongly Disagree

1. Do you understand your management processes today?
<--- Score

2. Were there any improvement opportunities identified from the process analysis?
<--- Score

3. Is there an established change management process?

<--- Score

4. What information qualified as important?
<--- Score

5. Do you, as a leader, bounce back quickly from setbacks?
<--- Score

6. How can risk management be tied procedurally to process elements?
<--- Score

7. How do you implement and manage your work processes to ensure that they meet design requirements?
<--- Score

8. What is the cost of poor quality as supported by the team's analysis?
<--- Score

9. How does the organization define, manage, and improve its Marketing Strategy and Execution processes?
<--- Score

10. Is the gap/opportunity displayed and communicated in financial terms?
<--- Score

11. How do you measure the operational performance of your key work systems and processes, including productivity, cycle time, and other appropriate measures of process effectiveness, efficiency, and innovation?

<--- Score

12. What is your organizations process which leads to recognition of value generation?
<--- Score

13. How do you define collaboration and team output?
<--- Score

14. Who is involved in the management review process?
<--- Score

15. Should you invest in industry-recognized qualifications?
<--- Score

16. What kind of crime could a potential new hire have committed that would not only not disqualify him/her from being hired by your organization, but would actually indicate that he/she might be a particularly good fit?
<--- Score

17. Has data output been validated?
<--- Score

18. What data do you need to collect?
<--- Score

19. What are the personnel training and qualifications required?
<--- Score

20. Are you missing Marketing Strategy and Execution

opportunities?
<--- Score

21. What tools were used to generate the list of possible causes?
<--- Score

22. Are gaps between current performance and the goal performance identified?
<--- Score

23. What does the data say about the performance of the stakeholder process?
<--- Score

24. What are evaluation criteria for the output?
<--- Score

25. How much data can be collected in the given timeframe?
<--- Score

26. What process should you select for improvement?
<--- Score

27. Do you have the authority to produce the output?
<--- Score

28. How is Marketing Strategy and Execution data gathered?
<--- Score

29. What qualifications and skills do you need?
<--- Score

30. What is your organizations system for selecting

qualified vendors?
<--- Score

31. Where can you get qualified talent today?
<--- Score

32. Who is involved with workflow mapping?
<--- Score

33. What qualifications are necessary?
<--- Score

34. What qualifications do Marketing Strategy and Execution leaders need?
<--- Score

35. Did any value-added analysis or 'lean thinking' take place to identify some of the gaps shown on the 'as is' process map?
<--- Score

36. What are the Marketing Strategy and Execution design outputs?
<--- Score

37. Which Marketing Strategy and Execution data should be retained?
<--- Score

38. What tools were used to narrow the list of possible causes?
<--- Score

39. What qualifies as competition?
<--- Score

40. What are your key performance measures or indicators and in-process measures for the control and improvement of your Marketing Strategy and Execution processes?
<--- Score

41. What is the oversight process?
<--- Score

42. How will corresponding data be collected?
<--- Score

43. What resources go in to get the desired output?
<--- Score

44. How do you ensure that the Marketing Strategy and Execution opportunity is realistic?
<--- Score

45. Is there a strict change management process?
<--- Score

46. What qualifications are needed?
<--- Score

47. What are the Marketing Strategy and Execution business drivers?
<--- Score

48. What were the financial benefits resulting from any 'ground fruit or low-hanging fruit' (quick fixes)?
<--- Score

49. Have you defined which data is gathered how?
<--- Score

50. How was the detailed process map generated, verified, and validated?
<--- Score

51. What systems/processes must you excel at?
<--- Score

52. Is the required Marketing Strategy and Execution data gathered?
<--- Score

53. What conclusions were drawn from the team's data collection and analysis? How did the team reach these conclusions?
<--- Score

54. Do your employees have the opportunity to do what they do best everyday?
<--- Score

55. Is the Marketing Strategy and Execution process severely broken such that a re-design is necessary?
<--- Score

56. What are your Marketing Strategy and Execution processes?
<--- Score

57. What is the complexity of the output produced?
<--- Score

58. How do you identify specific Marketing Strategy and Execution investment opportunities and emerging trends?
<--- Score

59. Are your outputs consistent?

<--- Score

60. Are Marketing Strategy and Execution changes recognized early enough to be approved through the regular process?

<--- Score

61. What controls do you have in place to protect data?

<--- Score

62. What are the best opportunities for value improvement?

<--- Score

63. A compounding model resolution with available relevant data can often provide insight towards a solution methodology; which Marketing Strategy and Execution models, tools and techniques are necessary?

<--- Score

64. Is the final output clearly identified?

<--- Score

65. Have any additional benefits been identified that will result from closing all or most of the gaps?

<--- Score

66. Are all staff in core Marketing Strategy and Execution subjects Highly Qualified?

<--- Score

67. What are the necessary qualifications?

<--- Score

68. What is the Value Stream Mapping?
<--- Score

69. Did any additional data need to be collected?
<--- Score

70. What Marketing Strategy and Execution metrics are outputs of the process?
<--- Score

71. Was a cause-and-effect diagram used to explore the different types of causes (or sources of variation)?
<--- Score

72. What Marketing Strategy and Execution data should be managed?
<--- Score

73. Think about some of the processes you undertake within your organization, which do you own?
<--- Score

74. Can you add value to the current Marketing Strategy and Execution decision-making process (largely qualitative) by incorporating uncertainty modeling (more quantitative)?
<--- Score

75. How is the way you as the leader think and process information affecting your organizational culture?
<--- Score

76. What did the team gain from developing a sub-process map?
<--- Score

77. Who owns what data?

<--- Score

78. What methods do you use to gather Marketing Strategy and Execution data?

<--- Score

79. What Marketing Strategy and Execution data should be collected?

<--- Score

80. What, related to, Marketing Strategy and Execution processes does your organization outsource?

<--- Score

81. How do mission and objectives affect the Marketing Strategy and Execution processes of your organization?

<--- Score

82. Who qualifies to gain access to data?

<--- Score

83. What quality tools were used to get through the analyze phase?

<--- Score

84. How will the change process be managed?

<--- Score

85. What successful thing are you doing today that may be blinding you to new growth opportunities?

<--- Score

86. Is the suppliers process defined and controlled?
<--- Score

87. What internal processes need improvement?
<--- Score

88. When should a process be art not science?
<--- Score

89. What are the processes for audit reporting and management?
<--- Score

90. Who gets your output?
<--- Score

91. How will the Marketing Strategy and Execution data be captured?
<--- Score

92. What training and qualifications will you need?
<--- Score

93. Is data and process analysis, root cause analysis and quantifying the gap/opportunity in place?
<--- Score

94. Do your leaders quickly bounce back from setbacks?
<--- Score

95. What are your current levels and trends in key Marketing Strategy and Execution measures or indicators of product and process performance that are important to and directly serve your

customers?

<--- Score

96. Do several people in different organizational units assist with the Marketing Strategy and Execution process?

<--- Score

97. Record-keeping requirements flow from the records needed as inputs, outputs, controls and for transformation of a Marketing Strategy and Execution process, are the records needed as inputs to the Marketing Strategy and Execution process available?

<--- Score

98. What are the disruptive Marketing Strategy and Execution technologies that enable your organization to radically change your business processes?

<--- Score

99. What are the revised rough estimates of the financial savings/opportunity for Marketing Strategy and Execution improvements?

<--- Score

100. What types of data do your Marketing Strategy and Execution indicators require?

<--- Score

101. How do you promote understanding that opportunity for improvement is not criticism of the status quo, or the people who created the status quo?

<--- Score

102. What data is gathered?

<--- Score

103. What other jobs or tasks affect the performance of the steps in the Marketing Strategy and Execution process?
<--- Score

104. What are your best practices for minimizing Marketing Strategy and Execution project risk, while demonstrating incremental value and quick wins throughout the Marketing Strategy and Execution project lifecycle?
<--- Score

105. What is the output?
<--- Score

106. Were Pareto charts (or similar) used to portray the 'heavy hitters' (or key sources of variation)?
<--- Score

107. How do you use Marketing Strategy and Execution data and information to support organizational decision making and innovation?
<--- Score

108. How is the Marketing Strategy and Execution Value Stream Mapping managed?
<--- Score

109. What are your outputs?
<--- Score

110. What were the crucial 'moments of truth' on the process map?
<--- Score

111. How often will data be collected for measures?
<--- Score

112. How are outputs preserved and protected?
<--- Score

113. How is the data gathered?
<--- Score

114. Is the performance gap determined?
<--- Score

115. Is pre-qualification of suppliers carried out?
<--- Score

116. What process improvements will be needed?
<--- Score

117. Do staff qualifications match your project?
<--- Score

118. What other organizational variables, such as reward systems or communication systems, affect the performance of this Marketing Strategy and Execution process?
<--- Score

119. How many input/output points does it require?
<--- Score

120. How has the Marketing Strategy and Execution data been gathered?
<--- Score

121. How difficult is it to qualify what Marketing Strategy and Execution ROI is?
<--- Score

122. What Marketing Strategy and Execution data will be collected?
<--- Score

123. Identify an operational issue in your organization, for example, could a particular task be done more quickly or more efficiently by Marketing Strategy and Execution?
<--- Score

124. Is there any way to speed up the process?
<--- Score

125. Were any designed experiments used to generate additional insight into the data analysis?
<--- Score

126. Was a detailed process map created to amplify critical steps of the 'as is' stakeholder process?
<--- Score

127. How do your work systems and key work processes relate to and capitalize on your core competencies?
<--- Score

128. What Marketing Strategy and Execution data do you gather or use now?
<--- Score

129. What are your current levels and trends in key measures or indicators of Marketing Strategy

and Execution product and process performance that are important to and directly serve your customers? How do these results compare with the performance of your competitors and other organizations with similar offerings?
<--- Score

130. How is data used for program management and improvement?
<--- Score

131. Have the problem and goal statements been updated to reflect the additional knowledge gained from the analyze phase?
<--- Score

132. Think about the functions involved in your Marketing Strategy and Execution project, what processes flow from these functions?
<--- Score

133. An organizationally feasible system request is one that considers the mission, goals and objectives of the organization, key questions are: is the Marketing Strategy and Execution solution request practical and will it solve a problem or take advantage of an opportunity to achieve company goals?
<--- Score

134. Who will gather what data?
<--- Score

135. Where is Marketing Strategy and Execution data gathered?
<--- Score

136. Who will facilitate the team and process?
<--- Score

137. Has an output goal been set?
<--- Score

138. Where is the data coming from to measure compliance?
<--- Score

Add up total points for this section:
_____ = Total points for this section

Divided by: _____ (number of statements answered) = _____
Average score for this section

Transfer your score to the Marketing Strategy and Execution Index at the beginning of the Self-Assessment.

CRITERION #5: IMPROVE:

INTENT: Develop a practical solution.
Innovate, establish and test the
solution and to measure the results.

In my belief, the answer to this
question is clearly defined:

5 Strongly Agree

4 Agree

3 Neutral

2 Disagree

1 Strongly Disagree

1. How can you improve performance?
<--- Score

2. Who are the Marketing Strategy and Execution
decision makers?
<--- Score

3. What is Marketing Strategy and Execution risk?
<--- Score

4. Is the solution technically practical?
<--- Score

5. How do you improve your likelihood of success ?
<--- Score

6. Can the solution be designed and implemented within an acceptable time period?
<--- Score

7. Have you identified breakpoints and/or risk tolerances that will trigger broad consideration of a potential need for intervention or modification of strategy?
<--- Score

8. In the past few months, what is the smallest change you have made that has had the biggest positive result? What was it about that small change that produced the large return?
<--- Score

9. What resources are required for the improvement efforts?
<--- Score

10. What tools were used to tap into the creativity and encourage 'outside the box' thinking?
<--- Score

11. For estimation problems, how do you develop an estimation statement?
<--- Score

12. What were the criteria for evaluating a Marketing

Strategy and Execution pilot?
<--- Score

13. What is the team's contingency plan for potential problems occurring in implementation?
<--- Score

14. Do the viable solutions scale to future needs?
<--- Score

15. What to do with the results or outcomes of measurements?
<--- Score

16. What tools were used to evaluate the potential solutions?
<--- Score

17. What actually has to improve and by how much?
<--- Score

18. Are events managed to resolution?
<--- Score

19. How do you go about comparing Marketing Strategy and Execution approaches/solutions?
<--- Score

20. What is Marketing Strategy and Execution's impact on utilizing the best solution(s)?
<--- Score

21. Is there a high likelihood that any recommendations will achieve their intended results?
<--- Score

22. How do you measure improved Marketing Strategy and Execution service perception, and satisfaction?
<--- Score

23. For decision problems, how do you develop a decision statement?
<--- Score

24. How can you better manage risk?
<--- Score

25. What risks do you need to manage?
<--- Score

26. How does the team improve its work?
<--- Score

27. Who controls the risk?
<--- Score

28. What needs improvement? Why?
<--- Score

29. How significant is the improvement in the eyes of the end user?
<--- Score

30. Have you achieved Marketing Strategy and Execution improvements?
<--- Score

31. Who will be responsible for documenting the Marketing Strategy and Execution requirements in detail?
<--- Score

32. How are policy decisions made and where?
<--- Score

33. What should a proof of concept or pilot accomplish?
<--- Score

34. Are the most efficient solutions problem-specific?
<--- Score

35. Are the key business and technology risks being managed?
<--- Score

36. What tools were most useful during the improve phase?
<--- Score

37. Who are the people involved in developing and implementing Marketing Strategy and Execution?
<--- Score

38. At what point will vulnerability assessments be performed once Marketing Strategy and Execution is put into production (e.g., ongoing Risk Management after implementation)?
<--- Score

39. What are the implications of the one critical Marketing Strategy and Execution decision 10 minutes, 10 months, and 10 years from now?
<--- Score

40. How do you define the solutions' scope?
<--- Score

41. How do you measure progress and evaluate training effectiveness?
<--- Score

42. What are your current levels and trends in key measures or indicators of workforce and leader development?
<--- Score

43. Is the Marketing Strategy and Execution risk managed?
<--- Score

44. What is the implementation plan?
<--- Score

45. How will you know that a change is an improvement?
<--- Score

46. Do you have the optimal project management team structure?
<--- Score

47. How will you know when its improved?
<--- Score

48. Is supporting Marketing Strategy and Execution documentation required?
<--- Score

49. Is any Marketing Strategy and Execution documentation required?
<--- Score

50. Do vendor agreements bring new compliance risk ?

<--- Score

51. Risk factors: what are the characteristics of Marketing Strategy and Execution that make it risky?

<--- Score

52. How can the phases of Marketing Strategy and Execution development be identified?

<--- Score

53. Does a good decision guarantee a good outcome?

<--- Score

54. Which Marketing Strategy and Execution solution is appropriate?

<--- Score

55. How does your organization evaluate strategic Marketing Strategy and Execution success?

<--- Score

56. How do you decide how much to remunerate an employee?

<--- Score

57. Are the risks fully understood, reasonable and manageable?

<--- Score

58. What are the Marketing Strategy and Execution security risks?

<--- Score

59. Who manages supplier risk management in your

organization?
<--- Score

60. Who will be using the results of the measurement activities?
<--- Score

61. What lessons, if any, from a pilot were incorporated into the design of the full-scale solution?
<--- Score

62. Can you integrate quality management and risk management?
<--- Score

63. How will you know that you have improved?
<--- Score

64. What Marketing Strategy and Execution improvements can be made?
<--- Score

65. How do you manage Marketing Strategy and Execution risk?
<--- Score

66. How do you deal with Marketing Strategy and Execution risk?
<--- Score

67. Who makes the Marketing Strategy and Execution decisions in your organization?
<--- Score

68. How do you improve Marketing Strategy and Execution service perception, and satisfaction?

<--- Score

69. What tools do you use once you have decided on a Marketing Strategy and Execution strategy and more importantly how do you choose?
<--- Score

70. Do you combine technical expertise with business knowledge and Marketing Strategy and Execution Key topics include lifecycles, development approaches, requirements and how to make a business case?
<--- Score

71. What alternative responses are available to manage risk?
<--- Score

72. Risk events: what are the things that could go wrong?
<--- Score

73. Where do you need Marketing Strategy and Execution improvement?
<--- Score

74. Was a Marketing Strategy and Execution charter developed?
<--- Score

75. Who manages Marketing Strategy and Execution risk?
<--- Score

76. What is the Marketing Strategy and Execution's sustainability risk?
<--- Score

77. Is the measure of success for Marketing Strategy and Execution understandable to a variety of people?
<--- Score

78. Risk Identification: What are the possible risk events your organization faces in relation to Marketing Strategy and Execution?
<--- Score

79. How is continuous improvement applied to risk management?
<--- Score

80. How will you recognize and celebrate results?
<--- Score

81. Who will be responsible for making the decisions to include or exclude requested changes once Marketing Strategy and Execution is underway?
<--- Score

82. Who are the Marketing Strategy and Execution decision-makers?
<--- Score

83. What practices helps your organization to develop its capacity to recognize patterns?
<--- Score

84. What are the expected Marketing Strategy and Execution results?
<--- Score

85. Are risk triggers captured?
<--- Score

86. How scalable is your Marketing Strategy and Execution solution?
<--- Score

87. How do you manage and improve your Marketing Strategy and Execution work systems to deliver customer value and achieve organizational success and sustainability?
<--- Score

88. What is the risk?
<--- Score

89. What criteria will you use to assess your Marketing Strategy and Execution risks?
<--- Score

90. Who should make the Marketing Strategy and Execution decisions?
<--- Score

91. How will you measure the results?
<--- Score

92. Would you develop a Marketing Strategy and Execution Communication Strategy?
<--- Score

93. How do you improve productivity?
<--- Score

94. What is the magnitude of the improvements?
<--- Score

95. What current systems have to be understood

and/or changed?
<--- Score

96. How do you mitigate Marketing Strategy and Execution risk?
<--- Score

97. Can you identify any significant risks or exposures to Marketing Strategy and Execution third- parties (vendors, service providers, alliance partners etc) that concern you?
<--- Score

98. Who do you report Marketing Strategy and Execution results to?
<--- Score

99. How can you improve Marketing Strategy and Execution?
<--- Score

100. Marketing Strategy and Execution risk decisions: whose call Is It?
<--- Score

101. Does the goal represent a desired result that can be measured?
<--- Score

102. What were the underlying assumptions on the cost-benefit analysis?
<--- Score

103. Is risk periodically assessed?
<--- Score

104. Which of the recognised risks out of all risks can be most likely transferred?
<--- Score

105. Are procedures documented for managing Marketing Strategy and Execution risks?
<--- Score

106. Do you cover the five essential competencies: Communication, Collaboration,Innovation, Adaptability, and Leadership that improve an organizations ability to leverage the new Marketing Strategy and Execution in a volatile global economy?
<--- Score

107. How can skill-level changes improve Marketing Strategy and Execution?
<--- Score

108. Is the scope clearly documented?
<--- Score

109. Explorations of the frontiers of Marketing Strategy and Execution will help you build influence, improve Marketing Strategy and Execution, optimize decision making, and sustain change, what is your approach?
<--- Score

110. What went well, what should change, what can improve?
<--- Score

111. What strategies for Marketing Strategy and Execution improvement are successful?

<--- Score

112. If you could go back in time five years, what decision would you make differently? What is your best guess as to what decision you're making today you might regret five years from now?
<--- Score

113. What do you want to improve?
<--- Score

114. How are Marketing Strategy and Execution risks managed?
<--- Score

115. How do you link measurement and risk?
<--- Score

116. What can you do to improve?
<--- Score

117. What improvements have been achieved?
<--- Score

118. When you map the key players in your own work and the types/domains of relationships with them, which relationships do you find easy and which challenging, and why?
<--- Score

119. Where do the Marketing Strategy and Execution decisions reside?
<--- Score

120. Who are the key stakeholders for the Marketing Strategy and Execution evaluation?

<--- Score

121. Who controls key decisions that will be made?
<--- Score

122. What are the affordable Marketing Strategy and Execution risks?

<--- Score

123. How do you keep improving Marketing Strategy and Execution?

<--- Score

124. Do those selected for the Marketing Strategy and Execution team have a good general understanding of what Marketing Strategy and Execution is all about?

<--- Score

125. Will the controls trigger any other risks?
<--- Score

126. What area needs the greatest improvement?
<--- Score

127. Are decisions made in a timely manner?
<--- Score

128. What are the concrete Marketing Strategy and Execution results?
<--- Score

129. Is Marketing Strategy and Execution documentation maintained?
<--- Score

Add up total points for this section:

_____ = Total points for this section

Divided by: _____ (number of
statements answered) = _____
Average score for this section

Transfer your score to the Marketing
Strategy and Execution Index at the
beginning of the Self-Assessment.

CRITERION #6: CONTROL:

INTENT: Implement the practical solution. Maintain the performance and correct possible complications.

In my belief, the answer to this question is clearly defined:

5 Strongly Agree

4 Agree

3 Neutral

2 Disagree

1 Strongly Disagree

1. Do you monitor the effectiveness of your Marketing Strategy and Execution activities?
<--- Score

2. Will existing staff require re-training, for example, to learn new business processes?
<--- Score

3. Is there a Marketing Strategy and Execution

Communication plan covering who needs to get what information when?
<--- Score

4. How will you measure your QA plan's effectiveness?
<--- Score

5. How do you select, collect, align, and integrate Marketing Strategy and Execution data and information for tracking daily operations and overall organizational performance, including progress relative to strategic objectives and action plans?
<--- Score

6. Are the planned controls working?
<--- Score

7. Can support from partners be adjusted?
<--- Score

8. How will the day-to-day responsibilities for monitoring and continual improvement be transferred from the improvement team to the process owner?
<--- Score

9. Is there a documented and implemented monitoring plan?
<--- Score

10. What is the standard for acceptable Marketing Strategy and Execution performance?
<--- Score

11. How will the process owner and team be able to hold the gains?

<--- Score

12. How might the group capture best practices and lessons learned so as to leverage improvements?
<--- Score

13. Has the Marketing Strategy and Execution value of standards been quantified?
<--- Score

14. Is there documentation that will support the successful operation of the improvement?
<--- Score

15. What are the key elements of your Marketing Strategy and Execution performance improvement system, including your evaluation, organizational learning, and innovation processes?
<--- Score

16. Have new or revised work instructions resulted?
<--- Score

17. Are the planned controls in place?
<--- Score

18. Will the team be available to assist members in planning investigations?
<--- Score

19. What is the best design framework for Marketing Strategy and Execution organization now that, in a post industrial-age if the top-down, command and control model is no longer relevant?
<--- Score

20. What adjustments to the strategies are needed?

<--- Score

21. What are you attempting to measure/monitor?

<--- Score

22. How do you plan on providing proper recognition and disclosure of supporting companies?

<--- Score

23. Does Marketing Strategy and Execution appropriately measure and monitor risk?

<--- Score

24. What other systems, operations, processes, and infrastructures (hiring practices, staffing, training, incentives/rewards, metrics/dashboards/scorecards, etc.) need updates, additions, changes, or deletions in order to facilitate knowledge transfer and improvements?

<--- Score

25. What quality tools were useful in the control phase?

<--- Score

26. Is a response plan established and deployed?

<--- Score

27. Are new process steps, standards, and documentation ingrained into normal operations?

<--- Score

28. Are you measuring, monitoring and predicting Marketing Strategy and Execution activities

to optimize operations and profitability, and enhancing outcomes?

<--- Score

29. Will any special training be provided for results interpretation?

<--- Score

30. Will your goals reflect your program budget?

<--- Score

31. Does a troubleshooting guide exist or is it needed?

<--- Score

32. Is there a recommended audit plan for routine surveillance inspections of Marketing Strategy and Execution's gains?

<--- Score

33. How will Marketing Strategy and Execution decisions be made and monitored?

<--- Score

34. What Marketing Strategy and Execution standards are applicable?

<--- Score

35. How is change control managed?

<--- Score

36. Do you monitor the Marketing Strategy and Execution decisions made and fine tune them as they evolve?

<--- Score

37. Has the improved process and its steps been

standardized?
<--- Score

38. How do you monitor usage and cost?
<--- Score

39. How likely is the current Marketing Strategy and Execution plan to come in on schedule or on budget?
<--- Score

40. How will the process owner verify improvement in present and future sigma levels, process capabilities?
<--- Score

41. Are documented procedures clear and easy to follow for the operators?
<--- Score

42. Do the Marketing Strategy and Execution decisions you make today help people and the planet tomorrow?
<--- Score

43. In the case of a Marketing Strategy and Execution project, the criteria for the audit derive from implementation objectives, an audit of a Marketing Strategy and Execution project involves assessing whether the recommendations outlined for implementation have been met, can you track that any Marketing Strategy and Execution project is implemented as planned, and is it working?
<--- Score

44. Is there a control plan in place for sustaining improvements (short and long-term)?
<--- Score

45. What do your reports reflect?

<--- Score

46. How do senior leaders actions reflect a commitment to the organizations Marketing Strategy and Execution values?

<--- Score

47. Is there a transfer of ownership and knowledge to process owner and process team tasked with the responsibilities.

<--- Score

48. How is Marketing Strategy and Execution project cost planned, managed, monitored?

<--- Score

49. What do you measure to verify effectiveness gains?

<--- Score

50. What do you stand for--and what are you against?

<--- Score

51. What is the recommended frequency of auditing?

<--- Score

52. What are your results for key measures or indicators of the accomplishment of your Marketing Strategy and Execution strategy and action plans, including building and strengthening core competencies?

<--- Score

53. Are the Marketing Strategy and Execution

standards challenging?
<--- Score

54. What key inputs and outputs are being measured on an ongoing basis?
<--- Score

55. Against what alternative is success being measured?
<--- Score

56. How do controls support value?
<--- Score

57. Is the Marketing Strategy and Execution test/ monitoring cost justified?
<--- Score

58. Is there a standardized process?
<--- Score

59. Implementation Planning: is a pilot needed to test the changes before a full roll out occurs?
<--- Score

60. What should the next improvement project be that is related to Marketing Strategy and Execution?
<--- Score

61. Where do ideas that reach policy makers and planners as proposals for Marketing Strategy and Execution strengthening and reform actually originate?
<--- Score

62. How widespread is its use?

<--- Score

63. Are operating procedures consistent?
<--- Score

64. Does the response plan contain a definite closed loop continual improvement scheme (e.g., plan-do-check-act)?
<--- Score

65. How will report readings be checked to effectively monitor performance?
<--- Score

66. How can you best use all of your knowledge repositories to enhance learning and sharing?
<--- Score

67. Act/Adjust: What Do you Need to Do Differently?
<--- Score

68. Are there documented procedures?
<--- Score

69. What are customers monitoring?
<--- Score

70. What other areas of the group might benefit from the Marketing Strategy and Execution team's improvements, knowledge, and learning?
<--- Score

71. What are the known security controls?
<--- Score

72. Who will be in control?

<--- Score

73. What is the control/monitoring plan?
<--- Score

74. Is knowledge gained on process shared and institutionalized?
<--- Score

75. Who controls critical resources?
<--- Score

76. Who has control over resources?
<--- Score

77. How do you spread information?
<--- Score

78. Is reporting being used or needed?
<--- Score

79. What is your theory of human motivation, and how does your compensation plan fit with that view?
<--- Score

80. How will input, process, and output variables be checked to detect for sub-optimal conditions?
<--- Score

81. Is new knowledge gained imbedded in the response plan?
<--- Score

82. How do you establish and deploy modified action plans if circumstances require a shift in plans and rapid execution of new plans?

<--- Score

83. Are pertinent alerts monitored, analyzed and distributed to appropriate personnel?
<--- Score

84. Are controls in place and consistently applied?
<--- Score

85. How will new or emerging customer needs/requirements be checked/communicated to orient the process toward meeting the new specifications and continually reducing variation?
<--- Score

86. What is your plan to assess your security risks?
<--- Score

87. Who is the Marketing Strategy and Execution process owner?
<--- Score

88. Are suggested corrective/restorative actions indicated on the response plan for known causes to problems that might surface?
<--- Score

89. Can you adapt and adjust to changing Marketing Strategy and Execution situations?
<--- Score

90. You may have created your quality measures at a time when you lacked resources, technology wasn't up to the required standard, or low service levels were the industry norm. Have those circumstances changed?

<--- Score

91. Is a response plan in place for when the input, process, or output measures indicate an 'out-of-control' condition?
<--- Score

92. Does job training on the documented procedures need to be part of the process team's education and training?
<--- Score

93. Does the Marketing Strategy and Execution performance meet the customer's requirements?
<--- Score

94. Is there an action plan in case of emergencies?
<--- Score

95. What should you measure to verify efficiency gains?
<--- Score

96. What are the critical parameters to watch?
<--- Score

97. Who is going to spread your message?
<--- Score

98. What can you control?
<--- Score

99. How do you plan for the cost of succession?
<--- Score

Add up total points for this section:

_____ = Total points for this section

Divided by: _____ (number of statements answered) = _____ Average score for this section

Transfer your score to the Marketing Strategy and Execution Index at the beginning of the Self-Assessment.

CRITERION #7: SUSTAIN:

INTENT: Retain the benefits.

In my belief, the answer to this question is clearly defined:

5 Strongly Agree

4 Agree

3 Neutral

2 Disagree

1 Strongly Disagree

1. What is the funding source for this project?
<--- Score

2. How do you stay inspired?
<--- Score

3. What are you challenging?
<--- Score

4. Who is on the team?
<--- Score

5. What one word do you want to own in the minds of your customers, employees, and partners?
<--- Score

6. What may be the consequences for the performance of an organization if all stakeholders are not consulted regarding Marketing Strategy and Execution?
<--- Score

7. Is maximizing Marketing Strategy and Execution protection the same as minimizing Marketing Strategy and Execution loss?
<--- Score

8. What happens if you do not have enough funding?
<--- Score

9. How do customers see your organization?
<--- Score

10. Operational - will it work?
<--- Score

11. If you were responsible for initiating and implementing major changes in your organization, what steps might you take to ensure acceptance of those changes?
<--- Score

12. Do Marketing Strategy and Execution rules make a reasonable demand on a users capabilities?
<--- Score

13. Have benefits been optimized with all key

stakeholders?
<--- Score

14. Is your strategy driving your strategy? Or is the way in which you allocate resources driving your strategy?
<--- Score

15. Is Marketing Strategy and Execution realistic, or are you setting yourself up for failure?
<--- Score

16. How do you foster the skills, knowledge, talents, attributes, and characteristics you want to have?
<--- Score

17. How will you insure seamless interoperability of Marketing Strategy and Execution moving forward?
<--- Score

18. Why is it important to have senior management support for a Marketing Strategy and Execution project?
<--- Score

19. Are assumptions made in Marketing Strategy and Execution stated explicitly?
<--- Score

20. How do you track customer value, profitability or financial return, organizational success, and sustainability?
<--- Score

21. How does Marketing Strategy and Execution integrate with other stakeholder initiatives?

<--- Score

22. Who will determine interim and final deadlines?
<--- Score

23. Which Marketing Strategy and Execution goals are the most important?
<--- Score

24. How do you transition from the baseline to the target?
<--- Score

25. How do you make it meaningful in connecting Marketing Strategy and Execution with what users do day-to-day?
<--- Score

26. Whose voice (department, ethnic group, women, older workers, etc) might you have missed hearing from in your company, and how might you amplify this voice to create positive momentum for your business?
<--- Score

27. If you do not follow, then how to lead?
<--- Score

28. What are the rules and assumptions your industry operates under? What if the opposite were true?
<--- Score

29. Who will be responsible for deciding whether Marketing Strategy and Execution goes ahead or not after the initial investigations?

<--- Score

30. Do you think you know, or do you know you know ?

<--- Score

31. If your customer were your grandmother, would you tell her to buy what you're selling?

<--- Score

32. What are specific Marketing Strategy and Execution rules to follow?

<--- Score

33. Is there any existing Marketing Strategy and Execution governance structure?

<--- Score

34. Do you have enough freaky customers in your portfolio pushing you to the limit day in and day out?

<--- Score

35. What is effective Marketing Strategy and Execution?

<--- Score

36. What is a feasible sequencing of reform initiatives over time?

<--- Score

37. Is Marketing Strategy and Execution dependent on the successful delivery of a current project?

<--- Score

38. Is there a work around that you can use?

<--- Score

39. Are you maintaining a past–present–future perspective throughout the Marketing Strategy and Execution discussion?

<--- Score

40. What would you recommend your friend do if he/she were facing this dilemma?

<--- Score

41. What happens at your organization when people fail?

<--- Score

42. Do you have past Marketing Strategy and Execution successes?

<--- Score

43. What are the challenges?

<--- Score

44. What are the essentials of internal Marketing Strategy and Execution management?

<--- Score

45. Who are four people whose careers you have enhanced?

<--- Score

46. What are current Marketing Strategy and Execution paradigms?

<--- Score

47. How much does Marketing Strategy and Execution help?

<--- Score

48. Can you maintain your growth without detracting from the factors that have contributed to your success?
<--- Score

49. If your company went out of business tomorrow, would anyone who doesn't get a paycheck here care?
<--- Score

50. What does your signature ensure?
<--- Score

51. Marketing budgets are tighter, consumers are more skeptical, and social media has changed forever the way we talk about Marketing Strategy and Execution, how do you gain traction?
<--- Score

52. What unique value proposition (UVP) do you offer?
<--- Score

53. What projects are going on in the organization today, and what resources are those projects using from the resource pools?
<--- Score

54. Are you satisfied with your current role? If not, what is missing from it?
<--- Score

55. How do you lead with Marketing Strategy and Execution in mind?
<--- Score

56. What stupid rule would you most like to kill?

<--- Score

57. How do you keep the momentum going?
<--- Score

58. Where can you break convention?
<--- Score

59. Who, on the executive team or the board, has spoken to a customer recently?
<--- Score

60. What counts that you are not counting?
<--- Score

61. What is your formula for success in Marketing Strategy and Execution ?
<--- Score

62. Have new benefits been realized?
<--- Score

63. Is your basic point _____ or _____?
<--- Score

64. Are you / should you be revolutionary or evolutionary?
<--- Score

65. Are you changing as fast as the world around you?
<--- Score

66. How do you accomplish your long range Marketing Strategy and Execution goals?
<--- Score

67. What management system can you use to leverage the Marketing Strategy and Execution experience, ideas, and concerns of the people closest to the work to be done?
<--- Score

68. What threat is Marketing Strategy and Execution addressing?
<--- Score

69. Do you feel that more should be done in the Marketing Strategy and Execution area?
<--- Score

70. Can the schedule be done in the given time?
<--- Score

71. To whom do you add value?
<--- Score

72. What is the kind of project structure that would be appropriate for your Marketing Strategy and Execution project, should it be formal and complex, or can it be less formal and relatively simple?
<--- Score

73. Why is Marketing Strategy and Execution important for you now?
<--- Score

74. What is your competitive advantage?
<--- Score

75. Can you do all this work?
<--- Score

76. What are the short and long-term Marketing Strategy and Execution goals?
<--- Score

77. What was the last experiment you ran?
<--- Score

78. Which models, tools and techniques are necessary?
<--- Score

79. Is the Marketing Strategy and Execution organization completing tasks effectively and efficiently?
<--- Score

80. What are the usability implications of Marketing Strategy and Execution actions?
<--- Score

81. How long will it take to change?
<--- Score

82. What is your BATNA (best alternative to a negotiated agreement)?
<--- Score

83. What are the success criteria that will indicate that Marketing Strategy and Execution objectives have been met and the benefits delivered?
<--- Score

84. What will be the consequences to the stakeholder (financial, reputation etc) if Marketing Strategy and Execution does not go ahead or fails to deliver the objectives?

<--- Score

85. What is the overall talent health of your organization as a whole at senior levels, and for each organization reporting to a member of the Senior Leadership Team?
<--- Score

86. Whom among your colleagues do you trust, and for what?
<--- Score

87. How can you negotiate Marketing Strategy and Execution successfully with a stubborn boss, an irate client, or a deceitful coworker?
<--- Score

88. Is there any reason to believe the opposite of my current belief?
<--- Score

89. Do you have an implicit bias for capital investments over people investments?
<--- Score

90. Political -is anyone trying to undermine this project?
<--- Score

91. What are the potential basics of Marketing Strategy and Execution fraud?
<--- Score

92. What trouble can you get into?
<--- Score

93. Why should you adopt a Marketing Strategy and Execution framework?
<--- Score

94. Will there be any necessary staff changes (redundancies or new hires)?
<--- Score

95. What role does communication play in the success or failure of a Marketing Strategy and Execution project?
<--- Score

96. What would have to be true for the option on the table to be the best possible choice?
<--- Score

97. How do you cross-sell and up-sell your Marketing Strategy and Execution success?
<--- Score

98. Are your responses positive or negative?
<--- Score

99. Do you have the right capabilities and capacities?
<--- Score

100. What potential megatrends could make your business model obsolete?
<--- Score

101. What is an unauthorized commitment?
<--- Score

102. Who do we want your customers to become?

<--- Score

103. What are the gaps in your knowledge and experience?
<--- Score

104. Are you making progress, and are you making progress as Marketing Strategy and Execution leaders?
<--- Score

105. What Marketing Strategy and Execution modifications can you make work for you?
<--- Score

106. Who do you think the world wants your organization to be?
<--- Score

107. Who will provide the final approval of Marketing Strategy and Execution deliverables?
<--- Score

108. What are internal and external Marketing Strategy and Execution relations?
<--- Score

109. Do you say no to customers for no reason?
<--- Score

110. How will you ensure you get what you expected?
<--- Score

111. What goals did you miss?
<--- Score

112. If you had to rebuild your organization without any traditional competitive advantages (i.e., no killer technology, promising research, innovative product/ service delivery model, etcetera), how would your people have to approach their work and collaborate together in order to create the necessary conditions for success?

<--- Score

113. What business benefits will Marketing Strategy and Execution goals deliver if achieved?

<--- Score

114. What are the long-term Marketing Strategy and Execution goals?

<--- Score

115. How do you keep records, of what?

<--- Score

116. What should you stop doing?

<--- Score

117. How do you deal with Marketing Strategy and Execution changes?

<--- Score

118. How do you foster innovation?

<--- Score

119. Ask yourself: how would you do this work if you only had one staff member to do it?

<--- Score

120. Is it economical; do you have the time and

money?
<--- Score

121. Do you think Marketing Strategy and Execution accomplishes the goals you expect it to accomplish?
<--- Score

122. What is the purpose of Marketing Strategy and Execution in relation to the mission?
<--- Score

123. At what moment would you think; Will I get fired?
<--- Score

124. Are the assumptions believable and achievable?
<--- Score

125. What are the key enablers to make this Marketing Strategy and Execution move?
<--- Score

126. Are new benefits received and understood?
<--- Score

127. Are you paying enough attention to the partners your company depends on to succeed?
<--- Score

128. What is the recommended frequency of auditing?
<--- Score

129. What Marketing Strategy and Execution skills are most important?
<--- Score

130. What is your question? Why?
<--- Score

131. In a project to restructure Marketing Strategy and Execution outcomes, which stakeholders would you involve?
<--- Score

132. Which individuals, teams or departments will be involved in Marketing Strategy and Execution?
<--- Score

133. Who is responsible for ensuring appropriate resources (time, people and money) are allocated to Marketing Strategy and Execution?
<--- Score

134. What have you done to protect your business from competitive encroachment?
<--- Score

135. Who will manage the integration of tools?
<--- Score

136. Why not do Marketing Strategy and Execution?
<--- Score

137. Why will customers want to buy your organizations products/services?
<--- Score

138. How can you become the company that would put you out of business?
<--- Score

139. What are the top 3 things at the forefront of your Marketing Strategy and Execution agendas for the next 3 years?
<--- Score

140. How do you create buy-in?
<--- Score

141. What is your Marketing Strategy and Execution strategy?
<--- Score

142. What did you miss in the interview for the worst hire you ever made?
<--- Score

143. Why do and why don't your customers like your organization?
<--- Score

144. How likely is it that a customer would recommend your company to a friend or colleague?
<--- Score

145. How do you determine the key elements that affect Marketing Strategy and Execution workforce satisfaction, how are these elements determined for different workforce groups and segments?
<--- Score

146. How do you govern and fulfill your societal responsibilities?
<--- Score

147. If there were zero limitations, what would you do differently?

<--- Score

148. How do you ensure that implementations of Marketing Strategy and Execution products are done in a way that ensures safety?
<--- Score

149. What is the big Marketing Strategy and Execution idea?
<--- Score

150. How do you set Marketing Strategy and Execution stretch targets and how do you get people to not only participate in setting these stretch targets but also that they strive to achieve these?
<--- Score

151. What are you trying to prove to yourself, and how might it be hijacking your life and business success?
<--- Score

152. Who do you want your customers to become?
<--- Score

153. What information is critical to your organization that your executives are ignoring?
<--- Score

154. How do you know if you are successful?
<--- Score

155. What you are going to do to affect the numbers?
<--- Score

156. What are your most important goals for the strategic Marketing Strategy and Execution objectives?
<--- Score

157. What must you excel at?
<--- Score

158. What is the source of the strategies for Marketing Strategy and Execution strengthening and reform?
<--- Score

159. Who is the main stakeholder, with ultimate responsibility for driving Marketing Strategy and Execution forward?
<--- Score

160. Instead of going to current contacts for new ideas, what if you reconnected with dormant contacts--the people you used to know? If you were going reactivate a dormant tie, who would it be?
<--- Score

161. Do you see more potential in people than they do in themselves?
<--- Score

162. What new services of functionality will be implemented next with Marketing Strategy and Execution ?
<--- Score

163. What is the range of capabilities?
<--- Score

164. How important is Marketing Strategy and

Execution to the user organizations mission?
<--- Score

165. Do you know who is a friend or a foe?
<--- Score

166. How much contingency will be available in the budget?
<--- Score

167. Has implementation been effective in reaching specified objectives so far?
<--- Score

168. In the past year, what have you done (or could you have done) to increase the accurate perception of your company/brand as ethical and honest?
<--- Score

169. How will you motivate the stakeholders with the least vested interest?
<--- Score

170. Is a Marketing Strategy and Execution breakthrough on the horizon?
<--- Score

171. How do you listen to customers to obtain actionable information?
<--- Score

172. Think of your Marketing Strategy and Execution project, what are the main functions?
<--- Score

173. How do you manage Marketing Strategy and

Execution Knowledge Management (KM)?
<--- Score

174. Why should people listen to you?
<--- Score

175. What knowledge, skills and characteristics mark a good Marketing Strategy and Execution project manager?
<--- Score

176. If no one would ever find out about your accomplishments, how would you lead differently?
<--- Score

177. What are the barriers to increased Marketing Strategy and Execution production?
<--- Score

178. How do you go about securing Marketing Strategy and Execution?
<--- Score

179. How can you incorporate support to ensure safe and effective use of Marketing Strategy and Execution into the services that you provide?
<--- Score

180. Who else should you help?
<--- Score

181. Are the criteria for selecting recommendations stated?
<--- Score

182. How can you become more high-tech but still

be high touch?
<--- Score

183. What do we do when new problems arise?
<--- Score

184. What is it like to work for you?
<--- Score

185. Which functions and people interact with the supplier and or customer?
<--- Score

186. If you find that you havent accomplished one of the goals for one of the steps of the Marketing Strategy and Execution strategy, what will you do to fix it?
<--- Score

187. Who is responsible for errors?
<--- Score

188. What have been your experiences in defining long range Marketing Strategy and Execution goals?
<--- Score

189. Will it be accepted by users?
<--- Score

190. Do you know what you are doing? And who do you call if you don't?
<--- Score

191. How is implementation research currently incorporated into each of your goals?
<--- Score

192. What relationships among Marketing Strategy and Execution trends do you perceive?
<--- Score

193. How do you provide a safe environment -physically and emotionally?
<--- Score

194. Who have you, as a company, historically been when you've been at your best?
<--- Score

195. Is a Marketing Strategy and Execution team work effort in place?
<--- Score

196. What happens when a new employee joins the organization?
<--- Score

197. What are strategies for increasing support and reducing opposition?
<--- Score

198. What is the estimated value of the project?
<--- Score

199. Are all key stakeholders present at all Structured Walkthroughs?
<--- Score

200. Would you rather sell to knowledgeable and informed customers or to uninformed customers?
<--- Score

201. Who are your customers?

<--- Score

202. Were lessons learned captured and communicated?

<--- Score

203. If you got fired and a new hire took your place, what would she do different?

<--- Score

204. If you had to leave your organization for a year and the only communication you could have with employees/colleagues was a single paragraph, what would you write?

<--- Score

205. How do you proactively clarify deliverables and Marketing Strategy and Execution quality expectations?

<--- Score

206. Are there any activities that you can take off your to do list?

<--- Score

207. Is the impact that Marketing Strategy and Execution has shown?

<--- Score

208. Do you have the right people on the bus?

<--- Score

209. Are you using a design thinking approach and integrating Innovation, Marketing Strategy and Execution Experience, and Brand Value?

<--- Score

210. Who uses your product in ways you never expected?
<--- Score

211. In retrospect, of the projects that you pulled the plug on, what percent do you wish had been allowed to keep going, and what percent do you wish had ended earlier?
<--- Score

212. How do you assess the Marketing Strategy and Execution pitfalls that are inherent in implementing it?
<--- Score

213. What are your personal philosophies regarding Marketing Strategy and Execution and how do they influence your work?
<--- Score

214. What trophy do you want on your mantle?
<--- Score

215. If you weren't already in this business, would you enter it today? And if not, what are you going to do about it?
<--- Score

216. Who are the key stakeholders?
<--- Score

Add up total points for this section:
_____ = Total points for this section

Divided by: _ _ _ _ _ _ (number of
statements answered) = _ _ _ _ _ _
Average score for this section

Transfer your score to the Marketing
Strategy and Execution Index at the
beginning of the Self-Assessment.

Marketing Strategy And Execution and Managing Projects, Criteria for Project Managers:

1.0 Initiating Process Group: Marketing Strategy And Execution

1. What will be the pressing issues of tomorrow?

2. What do they need to know about the Marketing Strategy And Execution project?

3. What areas does the group agree are the biggest success on the Marketing Strategy And Execution project?

4. When will the Marketing Strategy And Execution project be done?

5. How is each deliverable reviewed, verified, and validated?

6. What are the overarching issues of your organization?

7. First of all, should any action be taken?

8. During which stage of Risk planning are modeling techniques used to determine overall effects of risks on Marketing Strategy And Execution project objectives for high probability, high impact risks?

9. Are the changes in your Marketing Strategy And Execution project being formally requested, analyzed, and approved by the appropriate decision makers?

10. Realistic - are the desired results expressed in a way that the team will be motivated and believe that the required level of involvement will be obtained?

11. Does the Marketing Strategy And Execution project team have enough people to execute the Marketing Strategy And Execution project plan?

12. When must it be done?

13. Have you evaluated the teams performance and asked for feedback?

14. What is the NEXT thing to do?

15. How should needs be met?

16. Who is behind the Marketing Strategy And Execution project?

17. Who does what?

18. How well did you do?

19. In which Marketing Strategy And Execution project management process group is the detailed Marketing Strategy And Execution project budget created?

20. At which stage, in a typical Marketing Strategy And Execution project do stake holders have maximum influence?

1.1 Project Charter: Marketing Strategy And Execution

21. What is the justification?

22. Is it an improvement over existing products?

23. How will you know that a change is an improvement?

24. What outcome, in measureable terms, are you hoping to accomplish?

25. Customer: who are you doing the Marketing Strategy And Execution project for?

26. Does the Marketing Strategy And Execution project need to consider any special capacity or capability issues?

27. What are you striving to accomplish (measurable goal(s))?

28. Why have you chosen the aim you have set forth?

29. How high should you set your goals?

30. Who ise input and support will this Marketing Strategy And Execution project require?

31. Why do you need to manage scope?

32. What changes can you make to improve?

33. How will you learn more about the process or system you are trying to improve?

34. Will this replace an existing product?

35. Must Have?

36. Who is the Marketing Strategy And Execution project Manager?

37. What barriers do you predict to your success?

38. Who are the stakeholders?

39. Review the general mission What system will be affected by the improvement efforts?

40. Who is the sponsor?

1.2 Stakeholder Register: Marketing Strategy And Execution

41. How will reports be created?

42. What & Why?

43. Who wants to talk about Security?

44. How should employers make voices heard?

45. What opportunities exist to provide communications?

46. What is the power of the stakeholder?

47. Who is managing stakeholder engagement?

48. Is your organization ready for change?

49. What are the major Marketing Strategy And Execution project milestones requiring communications or providing communications opportunities?

50. How much influence do they have on the Marketing Strategy And Execution project?

51. How big is the gap?

1.3 Stakeholder Analysis Matrix: Marketing Strategy And Execution

52. Technology development and innovation?

53. Is changing technology threatening your organizations position?

54. Who is influential in the Marketing Strategy And Execution project area (both thematic and geographic areas)?

55. Competitor intentions - various?

56. Political effects?

57. How to involve media?

58. How can you fill the need to show progress?

59. Who holds positions of responsibility in interested organizations?

60. New markets, vertical, horizontal?

61. Organizational Applicability?

62. Insurmountable weaknesses?

63. How will the stakeholder directly benefit from the Marketing Strategy And Execution project and how will this affect the stakeholders motivation?

64. Benefit to whom?

65. What is the stakeholders power and status in relation to the Marketing Strategy And Execution project?

66. What tools would help you communicate?

67. Arena: in what fields are the actors active, where are they present?

68. Who will obstruct/hinder the Marketing Strategy And Execution project if they are not involved?

69. Contributions to policy and practice?

70. Cashflow, start-up cash-drain?

71. New technologies, services, ideas?

2.0 Planning Process Group: Marketing Strategy And Execution

72. How does activity resource estimation affect activity duration estimation?

73. In what way has the Marketing Strategy And Execution project come up with innovative measures for problem-solving?

74. The Marketing Strategy And Execution project charter is created in which Marketing Strategy And Execution project management process group?

75. You did your readings, yes?

76. What types of differentiated effects are resulting from the Marketing Strategy And Execution project and to what extent?

77. Just how important is your work to the overall success of the Marketing Strategy And Execution project?

78. What type of estimation method are you using?

79. Why is it important to determine activity sequencing on Marketing Strategy And Execution projects?

80. Who are the Marketing Strategy And Execution project stakeholders?

81. In what ways can the governance of the Marketing Strategy And Execution project be improved so that it has greater likelihood of achieving future sustainability?

82. To what extent has the intervention strategy been adapted to the areas of intervention in which it is being implemented?

83. If a task is partitionable, is this a sufficient condition to reduce the Marketing Strategy And Execution project duration?

84. To what extent has a PMO contributed to raising the quality of the design of the Marketing Strategy And Execution project?

85. How will you do it?

86. How can you make your needs known?

87. If you are late, will anybody notice?

88. What should you do next?

89. Do the partners have sufficient financial capacity to keep up the benefits produced by the programme?

90. What input will you be required to provide the Marketing Strategy And Execution project team?

91. What do you need to do?

2.1 Project Management Plan: Marketing Strategy And Execution

92. How do you manage integration?

93. What would you do differently what did not work?

94. What are the assigned resources?

95. Where does all this information come from?

96. How do you organize the costs in the Marketing Strategy And Execution project management plan?

97. What are the known stakeholder requirements?

98. If the Marketing Strategy And Execution project is complex or scope is specialized, do you have appropriate and/or qualified staff available to perform the tasks?

99. Why Change?

100. What did not work so well?

101. Is there an incremental analysis/cost effectiveness analysis of proposed mitigation features based on an approved method and using an accepted model?

102. What went right?

103. Is there anything you would now do differently

on your Marketing Strategy And Execution project based on past experience?

104. Do the proposed changes from the Marketing Strategy And Execution project include any significant risks to safety?

105. Are there any windfall benefits that would accrue to the Marketing Strategy And Execution project sponsor or other parties?

106. Do there need to be organizational changes?

107. Is mitigation authorized or recommended?

108. What data/reports/tools/etc. do program managers need?

109. Are there any scope changes proposed for a previously authorized Marketing Strategy And Execution project?

2.2 Scope Management Plan: Marketing Strategy And Execution

110. Have adequate resources been provided by management to ensure Marketing Strategy And Execution project success?

111. Are Marketing Strategy And Execution project team members involved in detailed estimating and scheduling?

112. Are the quality tools and methods identified in the Quality Plan appropriate to the Marketing Strategy And Execution project?

113. Is there a set of procedures defining the scope, procedures, and deliverables defining quality control?

114. Are all payments made according to the contract(s)?

115. Have Marketing Strategy And Execution project success criteria been defined?

116. Is the quality assurance team identified?

117. Are the results of quality assurance reviews provided to affected groups & individuals?

118. Are staffing resource estimates sufficiently detailed and documented for use in planning and tracking the Marketing Strategy And Execution project?

119. Is there a Steering Committee in place?

120. Staffing Requirements?

121. Is each item clearly and completely defined?

122. Pop quiz – what changed on Marketing Strategy And Execution project scope statement input?

123. Are trade-offs between accepting the risk and mitigating the risk identified?

124. Have all team members been part of identifying risks?

125. Are Marketing Strategy And Execution project contact logs kept up to date?

126. Describe the manner in which Marketing Strategy And Execution project deliverables will be formally presented and accepted. Will they be presented at the end of each phase?

127. Are changes in deliverable commitments agreed to by all affected groups & individuals?

128. Does the implementation plan have an appropriate division of responsibilities?

2.3 Requirements Management Plan: Marketing Strategy And Execution

129. What are you counting on?

130. Are all the stakeholders ready for the transition into the user community?

131. Should you include sub-activities?

132. Why manage requirements?

133. Will the product release be stable and mature enough to be deployed in the user community?

134. Do you have an appropriate arrangement for meetings?

135. Who is responsible for monitoring and tracking the Marketing Strategy And Execution project requirements?

136. Who came up with this requirement?

137. Is it new or replacing an existing business system or process?

138. Is requirements work dependent on any other specific Marketing Strategy And Execution project or non-Marketing Strategy And Execution project activities (e.g. funding, approvals, procurement)?

139. Have stakeholders been instructed in the Change

Control process?

140. What cost metrics will be used?

141. After the requirements are gathered and set forth on the requirements register, theyre little more than a laundry list of items. Some may be duplicates, some might conflict with others and some will be too broad or too vague to understand. Describe how the requirements will be analyzed. Who will perform the analysis?

142. How do you know that you have done this right?

143. Did you avoid subjective, flowery or non-specific statements?

144. Did you distinguish the scope of work the contractor(s) will be required to do?

145. Will the contractors involved take full responsibility?

146. Do you have an agreed upon process for alerting the Marketing Strategy And Execution project Manager if a request for change in requirements leads to a product scope change?

147. Will you have access to stakeholders when you need them?

148. Do you really need to write this document at all?

2.4 Requirements Documentation: Marketing Strategy And Execution

149. How to document system requirements?

150. What kind of entity is a problem ?

151. What are the potential disadvantages/ advantages?

152. Is new technology needed?

153. What is your Elevator Speech?

154. Who is involved?

155. What if the system wasn t implemented?

156. How can you document system requirements?

157. What are the acceptance criteria?

158. Are there any requirements conflicts?

159. What is a show stopper in the requirements?

160. Are all functions required by the customer included?

161. Who is interacting with the system?

162. Do technical resources exist?

163. Is the origin of the requirement clearly stated?

164. Basic work/business process; high-level, what is being touched?

165. How will the proposed Marketing Strategy And Execution project help?

166. Can the requirement be changed without a large impact on other requirements?

167. Validity. does the system provide the functions which best support the customers needs?

168. What are current process problems?

2.5 Requirements Traceability Matrix: Marketing Strategy And Execution

169. Describe the process for approving requirements so they can be added to the traceability matrix and Marketing Strategy And Execution project work can be performed. Will the Marketing Strategy And Execution project requirements become approved in writing?

170. Will you use a Requirements Traceability Matrix?

171. What percentage of Marketing Strategy And Execution projects are producing traceability matrices between requirements and other work products?

172. How will it affect the stakeholders personally in career?

173. How small is small enough?

174. How do you manage scope?

175. Why do you manage scope?

176. Why use a WBS?

177. What are the chronologies, contingencies, consequences, criteria?

178. What is the WBS?

179. Is there a requirements traceability process in

place?

180. Do you have a clear understanding of all subcontracts in place?

2.6 Project Scope Statement: Marketing Strategy And Execution

181. Have the reports to be produced, distributed, and filed been defined?

182. How often do you estimate that the scope might change, and why?

183. What are the major deliverables of the Marketing Strategy And Execution project?

184. Will an issue form be in use?

185. Will the risk status be reported to management on a regular and frequent basis?

186. Is there a baseline plan against which to measure progress?

187. What are the possible consequences should a risk come to occur?

188. Will this process be communicated to the customer and Marketing Strategy And Execution project team?

189. Have the configuration management functions been assigned?

190. Are the meetings set up to have assigned note takers that will add action/issues to the issue list?

191. Are there backup strategies for key members of the Marketing Strategy And Execution project?

192. Any new risks introduced or old risks impacted. Are there issues that could affect the existing requirements for the result, service, or product if the scope changes?

193. What is the most common tool for helping define the detail?

194. Is the Marketing Strategy And Execution project sponsor function identified and defined?

195. Have you been able to easily identify success criteria and create objective measurements for each of the Marketing Strategy And Execution project scopes goal statements?

196. Is an issue management process documented and filed?

197. Elements that deal with providing the detail?

2.7 Assumption and Constraint Log: Marketing Strategy And Execution

198. Are there cosmetic errors that hinder readability and comprehension?

199. Does a documented Marketing Strategy And Execution project organizational policy & plan (i.e. governance model) exist?

200. Does a specific action and/or state that is known to violate security policy occur?

201. What do you log?

202. Are there unnecessary steps that are creating bottlenecks and/or causing people to wait?

203. Have Marketing Strategy And Execution project management standards and procedures been established and documented?

204. What if failure during recovery?

205. Are there procedures in place to effectively manage interdependencies with other Marketing Strategy And Execution projects / systems?

206. What worked well?

207. Are best practices and metrics employed to identify issues, progress, performance, etc.?

208. What does an audit system look like?

209. What strengths do you have?

210. Has a Marketing Strategy And Execution project Communications Plan been developed?

211. Does the document/deliverable meet all requirements (for example, statement of work) specific to this deliverable?

212. Is this model reasonable?

213. Does the Marketing Strategy And Execution project have a formal Marketing Strategy And Execution project Plan?

214. Have all necessary approvals been obtained?

215. Are there nonconformance issues?

216. Is the definition of the Marketing Strategy And Execution project scope clear; what needs to be accomplished?

2.8 Work Breakdown Structure: Marketing Strategy And Execution

217. How many levels?

218. How will you and your Marketing Strategy And Execution project team define the Marketing Strategy And Execution projects scope and work breakdown structure?

219. Why is it useful?

220. Do you need another level?

221. Is it still viable?

222. What has to be done?

223. How big is a work-package?

224. How far down?

225. Where does it take place?

226. Is the work breakdown structure (wbs) defined and is the scope of the Marketing Strategy And Execution project clear with assigned deliverable owners?

227. Can you make it?

228. When would you develop a Work Breakdown Structure?

229. How much detail?

230. What is the probability of completing the Marketing Strategy And Execution project in less that xx days?

231. Who has to do it?

232. What is the probability that the Marketing Strategy And Execution project duration will exceed xx weeks?

233. Why would you develop a Work Breakdown Structure?

234. When does it have to be done?

2.9 WBS Dictionary: Marketing Strategy And Execution

235. Are current budgets resulting from changes to the authorized work and/or internal replanning, reconcilable to original budgets for specified reporting items?

236. What is the goal?

237. Are records maintained to show how management reserves are used?

238. Are overhead cost budgets established for each organization which has authority to incur overhead costs?

239. Are internal budgets for authorized, and not priced changes based on the contractors resource plan for accomplishing the work?

240. Are the procedures for identifying indirect costs to incurring organizations, indirect cost pools, and allocating the costs from the pools to the contracts formally documented?

241. Is the anticipated (firm and potential) business base Marketing Strategy And Execution projected in a rational, consistent manner?

242. Does the contractors system provide unit costs, equivalent unit or lot costs in terms of labor, material, other direct, and indirect costs?

243. Evaluate the performance of operating organizations?

244. Where engineering standards or other internal work measurement systems are used, is there a formal relationship between corresponding values and work package budgets?

245. Knowledgeable Marketing Strategy And Execution projections of future performance?

246. How detailed should a Marketing Strategy And Execution project get?

247. The anticipated business volume?

248. Does the contractor have procedures which permit identification of recurring or non-recurring costs as necessary?

249. Do work packages reflect the actual way in which the work will be done and are they meaningful products or management-oriented subdivisions of a higher level element of work?

250. Is work progressively subdivided into detailed work packages as requirements are defined?

251. Are retroactive changes to direct costs and indirect costs prohibited except for the correction of errors and routine accounting adjustments?

252. Are estimates developed by Marketing Strategy And Execution project personnel coordinated with the already stated responsible for overall

management to determine whether required resources will be available according to revised planning?

253. Time-phased control account budgets?

2.10 Schedule Management Plan: Marketing Strategy And Execution

254. Has the Marketing Strategy And Execution project manager been identified?

255. Are corrective actions and variances reported?

256. Is a pmo (Marketing Strategy And Execution project management office) in place and provide oversight to the Marketing Strategy And Execution project?

257. Is a process for scheduling and reporting defined, including forms and formats?

258. Does the Marketing Strategy And Execution project have quality set of schedule BOEs?

259. Does the schedule have reasonable float?

260. Has a provision been made to reassess Marketing Strategy And Execution project risks at various Marketing Strategy And Execution project stages?

261. Is it standard practice to formally commit stakeholders to the Marketing Strategy And Execution project via agreements?

262. Have all unresolved risks been documented?

263. Are there checklists created to determine if all quality processes are followed?

264. Are changes in scope (deliverable commitments) agreed to by all affected groups & individuals?

265. Are software metrics formally captured, analyzed and used as a basis for other Marketing Strategy And Execution project estimates?

266. Is current scope of the Marketing Strategy And Execution project substantially different than that originally defined?

267. Is there an on-going process in place to monitor Marketing Strategy And Execution project risks?

268. Why conduct schedule analysis?

269. Is there an approved case?

270. Are metrics used to evaluate and manage Vendors?

271. Has the Marketing Strategy And Execution project scope been baselined?

272. Has the scope management document been updated and distributed to help prevent scope creep?

2.11 Activity List: Marketing Strategy And Execution

273. What is the LF and LS for each activity?

274. How will it be performed?

275. What is the total time required to complete the Marketing Strategy And Execution project if no delays occur?

276. What went well?

277. Are the required resources available or need to be acquired?

278. Is there anything planned that does not need to be here?

279. Who will perform the work?

280. How can the Marketing Strategy And Execution project be displayed graphically to better visualize the activities?

281. What did not go as well?

282. For other activities, how much delay can be tolerated?

283. In what sequence?

284. Is infrastructure setup part of your Marketing

Strategy And Execution project?

285. What went wrong?

286. How do you determine the late start (LS) for each activity?

287. When do the individual activities need to start and finish?

288. How difficult will it be to do specific activities on this Marketing Strategy And Execution project?

289. How much slack is available in the Marketing Strategy And Execution project?

290. What will be performed?

2.12 Activity Attributes: Marketing Strategy And Execution

291. Have constraints been applied to the start and finish milestones for the phases?

292. Can more resources be added?

293. How difficult will it be to do specific activities on this Marketing Strategy And Execution project?

294. What conclusions/generalizations can you draw from this?

295. How difficult will it be to complete specific activities on this Marketing Strategy And Execution project?

296. How much activity detail is required?

297. Were there other ways you could have organized the data to achieve similar results?

298. Do you feel very comfortable with your prediction?

299. How else could the items be grouped?

300. Where else does it apply?

301. Does your organization of the data change its meaning?

302. Are the required resources available?

303. Can you re-assign any activities to another resource to resolve an over-allocation?

304. Activity: what is Missing?

305. Would you consider either of corresponding activities an outlier?

306. How many days do you need to complete the work scope with a limit of X number of resources?

307. What is missing?

308. Has management defined a definite timeframe for the turnaround or Marketing Strategy And Execution project window?

2.13 Milestone List: Marketing Strategy And Execution

309. How difficult will it be to do specific activities on this Marketing Strategy And Execution project?

310. Continuity, supply chain robustness?

311. Timescales, deadlines and pressures?

312. Own known vulnerabilities?

313. Sustainable financial backing?

314. How will you get the word out to customers?

315. What background experience, skills, and strengths does the team bring to your organization?

316. How soon can the activity start?

317. What would happen if a delivery of material was one week late?

318. Vital contracts and partners?

319. What has been done so far?

320. Legislative effects?

321. Describe your organizations strengths and core competencies. What factors will make your organization succeed?

322. Information and research?

323. Marketing - reach, distribution, awareness?

324. Describe the industry you are in and the market growth opportunities. What is the market for your technology, product or service?

325. What is the market for your technology, product or service?

326. Which path is the critical path?

327. Can you derive how soon can the whole Marketing Strategy And Execution project finish?

2.14 Network Diagram: Marketing Strategy And Execution

328. What is your organizations history in doing similar activities?

329. What activities must follow this activity?

330. How confident can you be in your milestone dates and the delivery date?

331. What job or jobs could run concurrently?

332. Where do you schedule uncertainty time?

333. What to do and When?

334. What job or jobs follow it?

335. What activity must be completed immediately before this activity can start?

336. How difficult will it be to do specific activities on this Marketing Strategy And Execution project?

337. What must be completed before an activity can be started?

338. What are the Key Success Factors?

339. Are you on time?

340. What are the tools?

341. Review the logical flow of the network diagram. Take a look at which activities you have first and then sequence the activities. Do they make sense?

342. What is the probability of completing the Marketing Strategy And Execution project in less that xx days?

343. What activities must occur simultaneously with this activity?

344. Planning: who, how long, what to do?

345. What controls the start and finish of a job?

346. Can you calculate the confidence level?

2.15 Activity Resource Requirements: Marketing Strategy And Execution

347. Other support in specific areas?

348. What is the Work Plan Standard?

349. What are constraints that you might find during the Human Resource Planning process?

350. Which logical relationship does the PDM use most often?

351. Why do you do that?

352. Time for overtime?

353. How many signatures do you require on a check and does this match what is in your policy and procedures?

354. When does monitoring begin?

355. Do you use tools like decomposition and rolling-wave planning to produce the activity list and other outputs?

356. How do you handle petty cash?

357. Are there unresolved issues that need to be addressed?

358. How do you manage time?

359. Anything else?

2.16 Resource Breakdown Structure: Marketing Strategy And Execution

360. Why do you do it?

361. Who will be used as a Marketing Strategy And Execution project team member?

362. What are the requirements for resource data?

363. How should the information be delivered?

364. What is the difference between % Complete and % work?

365. Which resources should be in the resource pool?

366. What is Marketing Strategy And Execution project communication management?

367. What defines a successful Marketing Strategy And Execution project?

368. Changes based on input from stakeholders?

369. What is each stakeholders desired outcome for the Marketing Strategy And Execution project?

370. The list could probably go on, but, the thing that you would most like to know is, How long & How much?

371. Is predictive resource analysis being done?

372. Any changes from stakeholders?

373. What is the purpose of assigning and documenting responsibility?

374. Who is allowed to perform which functions?

2.17 Activity Duration Estimates: Marketing Strategy And Execution

375. Does a process exist to identify Marketing Strategy And Execution project roles, responsibilities and reporting relationships?

376. Would you rate yourself as being risk-averse, risk-neutral, or risk-seeking?

377. How difficult will it be to do specific activities on this Marketing Strategy And Execution project?

378. Account for the make-or-buy process and how to perform the financial calculations involved in the process. What are the main types of contracts if you do decide to outsource?

379. Do procedures exist describing how the Marketing Strategy And Execution project scope will be managed?

380. What tasks can take place concurrently?

381. Which is the BEST thing to do to try to complete a Marketing Strategy And Execution project two days earlier?

382. See what went wrong?

383. Is a formal written notice that the contract is complete provided to the seller?

384. Which does one need in order to complete schedule development?

385. Will additional funds be needed for hardware or software?

386. Who will be the main sponsor for it?

387. What is done after activity duration estimation?

388. How do you enter durations, link tasks, and view critical path information?

389. Are updates on work results collected and used as inputs to the performance reporting process?

390. What type of activity sequencing method is required for corresponding activities?

391. After how many days will the lease cost be the same as the purchase cost for the equipment?

392. Are the causes of all variances identified?

2.18 Duration Estimating Worksheet: Marketing Strategy And Execution

393. Will the Marketing Strategy And Execution project collaborate with the local community and leverage resources?

394. What questions do you have?

395. What are the critical bottleneck activities?

396. Why estimate time and cost?

397. Can the Marketing Strategy And Execution project be constructed as planned?

398. What is next?

399. Done before proceeding with this activity or what can be done concurrently?

400. How can the Marketing Strategy And Execution project be displayed graphically to better visualize the activities?

401. Is this operation cost effective?

402. Does the Marketing Strategy And Execution project provide innovative ways for stakeholders to overcome obstacles or deliver better outcomes?

403. What is an Average Marketing Strategy And Execution project?

404. Why estimate costs?

405. What work will be included in the Marketing Strategy And Execution project?

406. When does your organization expect to be able to complete it?

407. What info is needed?

408. What utility impacts are there?

409. When, then?

2.19 Project Schedule: Marketing Strategy And Execution

410. Are all remaining durations correct?

411. What is risk?

412. Are the original Marketing Strategy And Execution project schedule and budget realistic?

413. How do you know that youhave done this right?

414. The wbs is developed as part of a joint planning session. and how do you know that youhave done this right?

415. Understand the constraints used in preparing the schedule. Are activities connected because logic dictates the order in which others occur?

416. Why is this particularly bad?

417. To what degree is do you feel the entire team was committed to the Marketing Strategy And Execution project schedule?

418. Why is software Marketing Strategy And Execution project disaster so common?

419. Eliminate unnecessary activities. Are there activities that came from a template or previous Marketing Strategy And Execution project that are not applicable on this phase of this Marketing Strategy

And Execution project?

420. How do you use schedules?

421. How can you fix it?

422. How effectively were issues able to be resolved without impacting the Marketing Strategy And Execution project Schedule or Budget?

423. Are activities connected because logic dictates the order in which others occur?

424. Change management required?

425. Schedule/cost recovery?

426. Are procedures defined by which the Marketing Strategy And Execution project schedule may be changed?

427. Why do you think schedule issues often cause the most conflicts on Marketing Strategy And Execution projects?

2.20 Cost Management Plan: Marketing Strategy And Execution

428. Are the payment terms being followed?

429. What weaknesses do you have?

430. Are assumptions being identified, recorded, analyzed, qualified and closed?

431. Has a resource management plan been created?

432. Milestones – what are the key dates in executing the contract plan?

433. Are internal Marketing Strategy And Execution project status meetings held at reasonable intervals?

434. Are tasks tracked by hours?

435. Are issues raised, assessed, actioned, and resolved in a timely and efficient manner?

436. Have the key elements of a coherent Marketing Strategy And Execution project management strategy been established?

437. Are the key elements of a Marketing Strategy And Execution project Charter present?

438. Are decisions captured in a decisions log?

439. Have activity relationships and

interdependencies within tasks been adequately identified?

440. Cost estimate preparation – What cost estimates will be prepared during the Marketing Strategy And Execution project phases?

441. Is the structure for tracking the Marketing Strategy And Execution project schedule well defined and assigned to a specific individual?

442. Who will prepare the cost estimates?

443. Are meeting minutes captured and sent out after the meeting?

444. Is there an on-going process in place to monitor Marketing Strategy And Execution project risks?

445. Have Marketing Strategy And Execution project management standards and procedures been identified / established and documented?

2.21 Activity Cost Estimates: Marketing Strategy And Execution

446. How do you allocate indirect costs to activities?

447. Did the consultant work with local staff to develop local capacity?

448. Is there anything unique in this Marketing Strategy And Execution projects scope statement that will affect resources?

449. How difficult will it be to do specific tasks on the Marketing Strategy And Execution project?

450. What were things that you did well, and could improve, and how?

451. Specific - is the objective clear in terms of what, how, when, and where the situation will be changed?

452. What were things that you did very well and want to do the same again on the next Marketing Strategy And Execution project?

453. Was it performed on time?

454. How do you fund change orders?

455. Vac -variance at completion, how much over/ under budget do you expect to be?

456. What do you want to know about the stay to

know if costs were inappropriately high or low?

457. What is the Marketing Strategy And Execution projects sustainability strategy that will ensure Marketing Strategy And Execution project results will endure or be sustained?

458. Did the Marketing Strategy And Execution project team have the right skills?

459. The impact and what actions were taken?

460. Does the activity use a common approach or business function to deliver its results?

461. Maintenance Reserve?

462. How do you do activity recasts?

463. Were you satisfied with the work?

464. Were escalated issues resolved promptly?

2.22 Cost Estimating Worksheet: Marketing Strategy And Execution

465. What will others want?

466. What is the estimated labor cost today based upon this information?

467. Does the Marketing Strategy And Execution project provide innovative ways for stakeholders to overcome obstacles or deliver better outcomes?

468. What can be included?

469. What is the purpose of estimating?

470. Is the Marketing Strategy And Execution project responsive to community need?

471. Value pocket identification & quantification what are value pockets?

472. What additional Marketing Strategy And Execution project(s) could be initiated as a result of this Marketing Strategy And Execution project?

473. Ask: are others positioned to know, are others credible, and will others cooperate?

474. Identify the timeframe necessary to monitor progress and collect data to determine how the selected measure has changed?

475. Will the Marketing Strategy And Execution project collaborate with the local community and leverage resources?

476. How will the results be shared and to whom?

477. Is it feasible to establish a control group arrangement?

478. Can a trend be established from historical performance data on the selected measure and are the criteria for using trend analysis or forecasting methods met?

479. Who is best positioned to know and assist in identifying corresponding factors?

480. What costs are to be estimated?

481. What happens to any remaining funds not used?

2.23 Cost Baseline: Marketing Strategy And Execution

482. Is request in line with priorities?

483. Who will use corresponding metrics ?

484. Review your risk triggers -have your risks changed?

485. Eac -estimate at completion, what is the total job expected to cost?

486. Have all approved changes to the schedule baseline been identified and impact on the Marketing Strategy And Execution project documented?

487. What do you want to measure ?

488. How concrete were original objectives?

489. Escalation criteria met?

490. Are you meeting with your team regularly?

491. Has training and knowledge transfer of the operations organization been completed?

492. What is the reality?

493. Are procedures defined by which the cost baseline may be changed?

494. What is it ?

495. Has the Marketing Strategy And Execution project documentation been archived or otherwise disposed as described in the Marketing Strategy And Execution project communication plan?

496. What is the consequence?

497. Definition of done can be traced back to the definitions of what are you providing to the customer in terms of deliverables?

498. Is the cr within Marketing Strategy And Execution project scope?

499. How will cost estimates be used?

2.24 Quality Management Plan: Marketing Strategy And Execution

500. Would impacts defined serve as impediments?

501. How effectively was the Quality Management Plan applied during Marketing Strategy And Execution project Execution?

502. What are your results for key measures/indicators of accomplishment of organizational strategy?

503. What data do you gather/use/compile?

504. How are records kept in the office?

505. Is the process working, and people are not executing in compliance of the process?

506. How does your organization decide what to measure?

507. How does your organization establish and maintain customer relationships?

508. What key performance indicators does your organization use to measure, manage, and improve key processes?

509. Is there a procedure for this process?

510. How is staff trained?

511. How are calibration records kept?

512. What is the Difference Between a QMP and QAPP?

513. Were the right locations/samples tested for the right parameters?

514. How does your organization manage training and evaluate its effectiveness?

515. Does the plan conform to standards?

516. Modifications to the requirements?

517. Are you meeting the quality standards?

518. How does your organization ensure the reliability, accuracy, timeliness, security and accessibility of data and information?

2.25 Quality Metrics: Marketing Strategy And Execution

519. Who is willing to lead?

520. What are your organizations next steps?

521. How do you measure?

522. Have alternatives been defined in the event that failure occurs?

523. How do you communicate results and findings to upper management?

524. What do you measure?

525. What approved evidence based screening tools can be used?

526. Which are the right metrics to use?

527. Does risk analysis documentation meet standards?

528. What percentage are outcome-based?

529. What method of measurement do you use?

530. What are you trying to accomplish?

531. Was material distributed on time?

532. What metrics do you measure?

533. Have risk areas been identified?

534. Is there a set of procedures to capture, analyze and act on quality metrics?

535. Are applicable standards referenced and available?

536. Who notifies stakeholders of normal and abnormal results?

537. How exactly do you define when differences exist?

2.26 Process Improvement Plan: Marketing Strategy And Execution

538. If a process improvement framework is being used, which elements will help the problems and goals listed?

539. Are you making progress on the improvement framework?

540. Why quality management?

541. To elicit goal statements, do you ask a question such as, What do you want to achieve?

542. Where are you now?

543. Purpose of goal: the motive is determined by asking, why do you want to achieve this goal?

544. Does your process ensure quality?

545. What is the test-cycle concept?

546. Are you making progress on the goals?

547. Modeling current processes is great, and will you ever see a return on that investment?

548. Why do you want to achieve the goal?

549. What personnel are the change agents for your initiative?

550. What is the return on investment?

551. How do you manage quality?

552. Have the supporting tools been developed or acquired?

553. What personnel are the coaches for your initiative?

554. Everyone agrees on what process improvement is, right?

555. What is quality and how will you ensure it?

556. Has the time line required to move measurement results from the points of collection to databases or users been established?

2.27 Responsibility Assignment Matrix: Marketing Strategy And Execution

557. Is budgeted cost for work performed calculated in a manner consistent with the way work is planned?

558. Are the wbs and organizational levels for application of the Marketing Strategy And Execution projected overhead costs identified?

559. Does the Marketing Strategy And Execution project need to be analyzed further to uncover additional responsibilities?

560. What is the business need?

561. Evaluate the impact of schedule changes, work around, etc?

562. Is every signing-off responsibility and every communicating responsibility critically necessary?

563. What are some important Marketing Strategy And Execution project communications management tools?

564. The staff interests – is the group or the person interested in working for this Marketing Strategy And Execution project?

565. Is accountability placed at the lowest-possible level within the Marketing Strategy And Execution

project so that decisions can be made at that level?

566. Does the accounting system provide a basis for auditing records of direct costs chargeable to the contract?

567. What does wbs accomplish?

568. What simple tool can you use to help identify and prioritize Marketing Strategy And Execution project risks that is very low tech and high touch?

569. Wbs elements contractually specified for reporting of status (lowest level only)?

570. What do you do when people do not respond?

571. The total budget for the contract (including estimates for authorized and unpriced work)?

572. How do you manage remotely to staff in other Divisions?

573. Will too many Communicating responsibilities tangle the Marketing Strategy And Execution project in unnecessary communications?

574. Is it safe to say you can handle more work or that some tasks you are supposed to do arent worth doing?

575. Are too many reports done in writing instead of verbally?

2.28 Roles and Responsibilities: Marketing Strategy And Execution

576. Implementation of actions: Who are the responsible units?

577. Who is responsible for each task?

578. Are your policies supportive of a culture of quality data?

579. Concern: where are you limited or have no authority, where you can not influence?

580. How is your work-life balance?

581. Are your budgets supportive of a culture of quality data?

582. Is there a training program in place for stakeholders covering expectations, roles and responsibilities and any addition knowledge others need to be good stakeholders?

583. What expectations were NOT met?

584. Does your vision/mission support a culture of quality data?

585. What are your major roles and responsibilities in the area of performance measurement and assessment?

586. Are the quality assurance functions and related roles and responsibilities clearly defined?

587. Who is responsible for implementation activities and where will the functions, roles and responsibilities be defined?

588. Be specific; avoid generalities. Thank you and great work alone are insufficient. What exactly do you appreciate and why?

589. Are governance roles and responsibilities documented?

590. Accountabilities: what are the roles and responsibilities of individual team members?

591. Do the values and practices inherent in the culture of your organization foster or hinder the process?

592. Was the expectation clearly communicated?

593. Attainable / achievable: the goal is attainable; can you actually accomplish the goal?

594. What should you do now to ensure that you are meeting all expectations of your current position?

2.29 Human Resource Management Plan: Marketing Strategy And Execution

595. Has the budget been baselined?

596. Have external dependencies been captured in the schedule?

597. Has the schedule been baselined?

598. Is quality monitored from the perspective of the customers needs and expectations?

599. Has your organization readiness assessment been conducted?

600. Is Marketing Strategy And Execution project work proceeding in accordance with the original Marketing Strategy And Execution project schedule?

601. Are internal Marketing Strategy And Execution project status meetings held at reasonable intervals?

602. Have the procedures for identifying budget variances been followed?

603. Is a payment system in place with proper reviews and approvals?

604. What is this Marketing Strategy And Execution project aiming to achieve?

605. Are status reports received per the Marketing Strategy And Execution project Plan?

606. Have key stakeholders been identified?

607. Are updated Marketing Strategy And Execution project time & resource estimates reasonable based on the current Marketing Strategy And Execution project stage?

608. Does the schedule include Marketing Strategy And Execution project management time and change request analysis time?

609. Is a stakeholder management plan in place that covers topics?

2.30 Communications Management Plan: Marketing Strategy And Execution

610. Are you constantly rushing from meeting to meeting?

611. Timing: when do the effects of the communication take place?

612. How is this initiative related to other portfolios, programs, or Marketing Strategy And Execution projects?

613. In your work, how much time is spent on stakeholder identification?

614. Who are the members of the governing body?

615. Are others part of the communications management plan?

616. How often do you engage with stakeholders?

617. Can you think of other people who might have concerns or interests?

618. Which stakeholders can influence others?

619. Who is involved as you identify stakeholders?

620. Are there too many who have an interest in some aspect of your work?

621. Will messages be directly related to the release strategy or phases of the Marketing Strategy And Execution project?

622. Are there common objectives between the team and the stakeholder?

623. What is the stakeholders level of authority?

624. Who did you turn to if you had questions?

625. Is the stakeholder role recognized by your organization?

626. Do you prepare stakeholder engagement plans?

627. Do you then often overlook a key stakeholder or stakeholder group?

628. Why do you manage communications?

2.31 Risk Management Plan: Marketing Strategy And Execution

629. Are some people working on multiple Marketing Strategy And Execution projects?

630. How is the audit profession changing?

631. Does the Marketing Strategy And Execution project have the authority and ability to avoid the risk?

632. Is the customer willing to participate in reviews?

633. What are it-specific requirements?

634. What are some questions that should be addressed in a risk management plan?

635. Is a software Marketing Strategy And Execution project management tool available?

636. Do benefits and chances of success outweigh potential damage if success is not attained?

637. Can the Marketing Strategy And Execution project proceed without assuming the risk?

638. What can you do to minimize the impact if it does?

639. Risk categories: what are the main categories of risks that should be addressed on this Marketing

Strategy And Execution project?

640. Do requirements put excessive performance constraints on the product?

641. What are the chances the event will occur?

642. Maximize short-term return on investment?

643. Are Marketing Strategy And Execution project requirements stable?

644. Do the people have the right combinations of skills?

645. Risk may be made during which step of risk management?

646. Are the metrics meaningful and useful?

647. What are the cost, schedule and resource impacts of avoiding the risk?

2.32 Risk Register: Marketing Strategy And Execution

648. How often will the Risk Management Plan and Risk Register be formally reviewed, and by whom?

649. How are risks identified?

650. What further options might be available for responding to the risk?

651. Have other controls and solutions been implemented in other services which could be applied as an alternative to additional funding?

652. Are there any gaps in the evidence?

653. What should you do when?

654. Preventative actions - planned actions to reduce the likelihood a risk will occur and/or reduce the seriousness should it occur. What should you do now?

655. What is the appropriate level of risk management for this Marketing Strategy And Execution project?

656. Cost/benefit – how much will the proposed mitigations cost and how does this cost compare with the potential cost of the risk event/situation should it occur?

657. Contingency actions - planned actions to reduce the immediate seriousness of the risk when it does

occur. What should you do when?

658. What are the main aims, objectives of the policy, strategy, or service and the intended outcomes?

659. Can the likelihood and impact of failing to achieve corresponding recommendations and action plans be assessed?

660. Is further information required before making a decision?

661. How are risks graded?

662. What should you do now?

663. What are the assumptions and current status that support the assessment of the risk?

664. Why would you develop a risk register?

665. Who is going to do it?

666. Amongst the action plans and recommendations that you have to introduce are there some that could stop or delay the overall program?

2.33 Probability and Impact Assessment: Marketing Strategy And Execution

667. How realistic is the timing of introduction?

668. What kind of preparation would be required to do this?

669. What would be the effect of slippage?

670. What are the chances the risk event will occur?

671. What are its business ethics?

672. Is a software Marketing Strategy And Execution project management tool available?

673. Which role do you have in the Marketing Strategy And Execution project?

674. Do you have a consistent repeatable process that is actually used?

675. Are there any Marketing Strategy And Execution projects similar to this one in existence?

676. What will be cost of redeployment of personnel?

677. What action do you usually take against risks?

678. Risk data quality assessment - what is the quality of the data used to determine or assess the risk?

679. What should be the external organizations responsibility vis-à-vis total stake in the Marketing Strategy And Execution project?

680. Are staff committed for the duration of the Marketing Strategy And Execution project?

681. Do requirements demand the use of new analysis, design, or testing methods?

682. Who will be responsible for a slippage?

683. To what extent is the chosen technology maturing?

684. How risk averse are you?

685. What things might go wrong?

686. How are you working with risks?

2.34 Probability and Impact Matrix: Marketing Strategy And Execution

687. Brain storm – mind maps, what if?

688. Is the Marketing Strategy And Execution project cutting across the entire organization?

689. What are the chances the risk events will occur?

690. Have staff received necessary training?

691. How do you manage Marketing Strategy And Execution project Risk?

692. Does the customer have a solid idea of what is required?

693. Does the Marketing Strategy And Execution project team have experience with the technology to be implemented?

694. What should be done NEXT?

695. Economic to take on the Marketing Strategy And Execution project?

696. What are the probable external agencies to act as Marketing Strategy And Execution project manager?

697. What are the ways you measure and evaluate risks?

698. How would you assess the risk management process in the Marketing Strategy And Execution project?

699. Are Marketing Strategy And Execution project requirements stable?

700. What can you use the analyzed risks for?

701. During Marketing Strategy And Execution project executing, a team member identifies a risk that is not in the risk register. What should you do?

702. What is the likely future demand of the customer?

703. Can it be changed quickly?

704. What will be the likely incidence of conflict with neighboring Marketing Strategy And Execution projects?

2.35 Risk Data Sheet: Marketing Strategy And Execution

705. Potential for recurrence?

706. How can it happen?

707. What actions can be taken to eliminate or remove risk?

708. Whom do you serve (customers)?

709. What do you know?

710. How reliable is the data source?

711. What are the main threats to your existence?

712. What can happen?

713. How do you handle product safely?

714. During work activities could hazards exist?

715. Are new hazards created?

716. Is the data sufficiently specified in terms of the type of failure being analyzed, and its frequency or probability?

717. What are your core values?

718. What are you trying to achieve (Objectives)?

719. Who has a vested interest in how you perform as your organization (our stakeholders)?

720. What is the likelihood of it happening?

721. What was measured?

2.36 Procurement Management Plan: Marketing Strategy And Execution

722. If standardized procurement documents are needed, where can others be found?

723. Has a sponsor been identified?

724. Public engagement – did you get it right?

725. Pareto diagrams, statistical sampling, flow charting or trend analysis used quality monitoring?

726. How will multiple providers be managed?

727. Does the Marketing Strategy And Execution project have a Quality Culture?

728. Are change requests logged and managed?

729. Are non-critical path items updated and agreed upon with the teams?

730. Are the Marketing Strategy And Execution project plans updated on a frequent basis?

731. Is there a procurement management plan in place?

732. Is there any form of automated support for Issues Management?

733. Is an industry recognized mechanized support

tool(s) being used for Marketing Strategy And Execution project scheduling & tracking?

734. How will you coordinate Procurement with aspects of the Marketing Strategy And Execution project?

735. Have the key functions and capabilities been defined and assigned to each release or iteration?

2.37 Source Selection Criteria: Marketing Strategy And Execution

736. What evidence should be provided regarding proposal evaluations?

737. What should clarifications include?

738. How are clarifications and communications appropriately used?

739. What management structure does your organization consider as optimal for performing the contract?

740. How should oral presentations be evaluated?

741. What can not be disclosed?

742. What should be the contracting officers strategy?

743. How should the solicitation aspects regarding past performance be structured?

744. Are resultant proposal revisions allowed?

745. Are responses to considerations adequate?

746. Who is entitled to a debriefing?

747. How do you facilitate evaluation against published criteria?

748. Who is on the Source Selection Advisory Committee?

749. When is it appropriate to issue a DRFP?

750. In which phase of the acquisition process cycle does source qualifications reside?

751. Is the offeror pricing what is technically proposed?

752. What documentation is necessary regarding electronic communications?

753. What is price analysis and when should it be performed?

754. What are the guiding principles for developing an evaluation report?

755. Can you reasonably estimate total organization requirements for the coming year?

2.38 Stakeholder Management Plan: Marketing Strategy And Execution

756. Have Marketing Strategy And Execution project success criteria been defined?

757. Are formal code reviews conducted?

758. Was trending evident between reviews?

759. Describe the process that will be used to design, develop, review, accept, distribute and change outputs. Will all outputs delivered by the Marketing Strategy And Execution project follow the same process?

760. Have Marketing Strategy And Execution project management standards and procedures been identified / established and documented?

761. Have all documents been archived in a Marketing Strategy And Execution project repository for each release?

762. Are all vendor contracts closed out?

763. Have all involved Marketing Strategy And Execution project stakeholders and work groups committed to the Marketing Strategy And Execution project?

764. Is the schedule updated on a periodic basis?

765. Has the business need been clearly defined?

766. Does the Marketing Strategy And Execution project have a Quality Culture?

767. How are you doing/what can be done better?

768. Is there an issues management plan in place?

769. When would you develop a Marketing Strategy And Execution project Execution Plan?

770. Will all outputs delivered by the Marketing Strategy And Execution project follow the same process?

771. Are mitigation strategies identified?

2.39 Change Management Plan: Marketing Strategy And Execution

772. How do you know the requirements you documented are the right ones?

773. Do you need new systems?

774. Who will be the change levers?

775. What can you do to minimise misinterpretation and negative perceptions?

776. What would be an estimate of the total cost for the activities required to carry out the change initiative?

777. Who will fund the training?

778. Will the readiness criteria be met prior to the training roll out?

779. What method and medium would you use to announce a message?

780. What did the people around you say about it?

781. Has a training need analysis been carried out?

782. What new roles are needed?

783. Do the proposed users have access to the appropriate documentation?

784. What are the essentials of the message?

785. How frequently should you repeat the message?

786. When does it make sense to customize?

787. Who might be able to help you the most?

788. Who is the audience for change management activities?

789. What is the worst thing that can happen if you chose not to communicate this information?

790. What is going to be done differently?

3.0 Executing Process Group: Marketing Strategy And Execution

791. How will professionals learn what is expected from them what the deliverables are?

792. What communication items need improvement?

793. What are the key components of the Marketing Strategy And Execution project communications plan?

794. What are the challenges Marketing Strategy And Execution project teams face?

795. What are the critical steps involved with strategy mapping?

796. Is the Marketing Strategy And Execution project performing better or worse than planned?

797. Mitigate. what will you do to minimize the impact should a risk event occur?

798. When do you share the scorecard with managers?

799. Will outside resources be needed to help?

800. Is the schedule for the set products being met?

801. What are the main types of contracts if you do decide to outsource?

802. Who are the Marketing Strategy And Execution project stakeholders?

803. What are crucial elements of successful Marketing Strategy And Execution project plan execution?

804. How can your organization use a weighted decision matrix to evaluate proposals as part of source selection?

805. Are decisions made in a timely manner?

806. What are the main types of goods and services being outsourced?

807. What does it mean to take a systems view of a Marketing Strategy And Execution project?

808. Who will be the main sponsor?

809. What are the main parts of the scope statement?

810. Measurable - are the targets measurable?

3.1 Team Member Status Report: Marketing Strategy And Execution

811. How does this product, good, or service meet the needs of the Marketing Strategy And Execution project and your organization as a whole?

812. The problem with Reward & Recognition Programs is that the truly deserving people all too often get left out. How can you make it practical?

813. When a teams productivity and success depend on collaboration and the efficient flow of information, what generally fails them?

814. Are your organizations Marketing Strategy And Execution projects more successful over time?

815. Does the product, good, or service already exist within your organization?

816. Does your organization have the means (staff, money, contract, etc.) to produce or to acquire the product, good, or service?

817. Are the products of your organizations Marketing Strategy And Execution projects meeting customers objectives?

818. How can you make it practical?

819. Do you have an Enterprise Marketing Strategy And Execution project Management Office (EPMO)?

820. How much risk is involved?

821. Are the attitudes of staff regarding Marketing Strategy And Execution project work improving?

822. What specific interest groups do you have in place?

823. Why is it to be done?

824. How it is to be done?

825. Does every department have to have a Marketing Strategy And Execution project Manager on staff?

826. What is to be done?

827. Is there evidence that staff is taking a more professional approach toward management of your organizations Marketing Strategy And Execution projects?

828. How will resource planning be done?

829. Will the staff do training or is that done by a third party?

3.2 Change Request: Marketing Strategy And Execution

830. When to submit a change request?

831. How does your organization control changes before and after software is released to a customer?

832. How does a team identify the discrete elements of a configuration?

833. Who needs to approve change requests?

834. Screen shots or attachments included in a Change Request?

835. What has an inspector to inspect and to check?

836. When do you create a change request?

837. What are the duties of the change control team?

838. Has your address changed?

839. What needs to be communicated?

840. Are you implementing itil processes?

841. Will new change requests be acknowledged in a timely manner?

842. What are the basic mechanics of the Change Advisory Board (CAB)?

843. How shall the implementation of changes be recorded?

844. What can be filed?

845. What is the relationship between requirements attributes and reliability?

846. How are the measures for carrying out the change established?

847. How is quality being addressed on the Marketing Strategy And Execution project?

848. What is the purpose of change control?

3.3 Change Log: Marketing Strategy And Execution

849. When was the request approved?

850. Is the submitted change a new change or a modification of a previously approved change?

851. Do the described changes impact on the integrity or security of the system?

852. Is this a mandatory replacement?

853. Is the change backward compatible without limitations?

854. Will the Marketing Strategy And Execution project fail if the change request is not executed?

855. How does this change affect scope?

856. Is the change request open, closed or pending?

857. Where do changes come from?

858. Should a more thorough impact analysis be conducted?

859. Who initiated the change request?

860. Does the suggested change request seem to represent a necessary enhancement to the product?

861. Is the requested change request a result of changes in other Marketing Strategy And Execution project(s)?

862. Does the suggested change request represent a desired enhancement to the products functionality?

863. When was the request submitted?

864. Is the change request within Marketing Strategy And Execution project scope?

865. How does this change affect the timeline of the schedule?

866. How does this relate to the standards developed for specific business processes?

3.4 Decision Log: Marketing Strategy And Execution

867. What makes you different or better than others companies selling the same thing?

868. What alternatives/risks were considered?

869. What are the cost implications?

870. How effective is maintaining the log at facilitating organizational learning?

871. What is your overall strategy for quality control / quality assurance procedures?

872. Meeting purpose; why does this team meet?

873. It becomes critical to track and periodically revisit both operational effectiveness; Are you noticing all that you need to, and are you interpreting what you see effectively?

874. What eDiscovery problem or issue did your organization set out to fix or make better?

875. How do you define success?

876. Who will be given a copy of this document and where will it be kept?

877. Do strategies and tactics aimed at less than full control reduce the costs of management or simply

shift the cost burden?

878. Is everything working as expected?

879. What is the line where eDiscovery ends and document review begins?

880. Which variables make a critical difference?

881. How consolidated and comprehensive a story can you tell by capturing currently available incident data in a central location and through a log of key decisions during an incident?

882. Is your opponent open to a non-traditional workflow, or will it likely challenge anything you do?

883. At what point in time does loss become unacceptable?

884. Who is the decisionmaker?

885. How does the use a Decision Support System influence the strategies/tactics or costs?

886. Decision-making process; how will the team make decisions?

3.5 Quality Audit: Marketing Strategy And Execution

887. How does your organization know that its system for governing staff behaviour is appropriately effective and constructive?

888. How does your organization know that its systems for meeting staff extracurricular learning support requirements are appropriately effective and constructive?

889. It is inappropriate to seek information about the Audit Panels preliminary views including questions like why do you ask that?

890. Have personnel cleanliness and health requirements been established?

891. How does your organization know that its system for staff performance planning and review is appropriately effective and constructive?

892. How does your organization know that its staff support services planning and management systems are appropriately effective and constructive?

893. How does your organization know that the support for its staff is appropriately effective and constructive?

894. How does your organization know that its security arrangements are appropriately effective and

constructive?

895. How does your organization know that its system for examining work done is appropriately effective and constructive?

896. How does your organization know that its system for ensuring a positive organizational climate is appropriately effective and constructive?

897. Is there a written procedure for receiving materials?

898. Are there appropriate indicators for monitoring the effectiveness and efficiency of processes?

899. Are all records associated with the reconditioning of a device maintained for a minimum of two years after the sale or disposal of the last device within a lot of merchandise?

900. How does your organization know that its systems for providing high quality consultancy services to external parties are appropriately effective and constructive?

901. Quality is about improvement and accountability. The immediate questions that arise out of that statement are: (i) improvement on what, and (ii) accountable to whom?

902. What does the organizarion look for in a Quality audit?

903. How does your organization know that its systems for communicating with and among staff are

appropriately effective and constructive?

904. How does your organization know that its staffing profile is optimally aligned with the capability requirements implicit (or explicit) in its Strategic Plan?

905. What will the Observer get to Observe?

906. How does your organization know that its Strategic Plan is providing the best guidance for the future of your organization?

3.6 Team Directory: Marketing Strategy And Execution

907. How does the team resolve conflicts and ensure tasks are completed?

908. Where should the information be distributed?

909. How do unidentified risks impact the outcome of the Marketing Strategy And Execution project?

910. Process decisions: are contractors adequately prosecuting the work?

911. Timing: when do the effects of communication take place?

912. Decisions: is the most suitable form of contract being used?

913. Who should receive information (all stakeholders)?

914. Who will talk to the customer?

915. Who are your stakeholders (customers, sponsors, end users, team members)?

916. Who will be the stakeholders on your next Marketing Strategy And Execution project?

917. Process decisions: do job conditions warrant additional actions to collect job information and

document on-site activity?

918. Who will report Marketing Strategy And Execution project status to all stakeholders?

919. Why is the work necessary?

920. Is construction on schedule?

921. How will the team handle changes?

922. Process decisions: do invoice amounts match accepted work in place?

923. How and in what format should information be presented?

924. Process decisions: which organizational elements and which individuals will be assigned management functions?

925. Days from the time the issue is identified?

3.7 Team Operating Agreement: Marketing Strategy And Execution

926. How will your group handle planned absences?

927. Have you set the goals and objectives of the team?

928. Do you record meetings for the already stated unable to attend?

929. Did you recap the meeting purpose, time, and expectations?

930. Do you leverage technology engagement tools group chat, polls, screen sharing, etc.?

931. What individual strengths does each team member bring to the group?

932. What is a Virtual Team?

933. Do you brief absent members after they view meeting notes or listen to a recording?

934. To whom do you deliver your services?

935. Do you prevent individuals from dominating the meeting?

936. Have you established procedures that team members can follow to work effectively together, such as a team operating agreement?

937. Methodologies: how will key team processes be implemented, such as training, research, work deliverable production, review and approval processes, knowledge management, and meeting procedures?

938. Did you determine the technology methods that best match the messages to be communicated?

939. Are there the right people on your team?

940. Are there more than two functional areas represented by your team?

941. How do you want to be thought of and known within your organization?

942. What types of accommodations will be formulated and put in place for sustaining the team?

943. Do you post any action items, due dates, and responsibilities on the team website?

944. Has the appropriate access to relevant data and analysis capability been granted?

945. What are the current caseload numbers in the unit?

3.8 Team Performance Assessment: Marketing Strategy And Execution

946. Social categorization and intergroup behaviour: Does minimal intergroup discrimination make social identity more positive?

947. How hard do you try to make a good selection?

948. To what degree does the teams approach to its work allow for modification and improvement over time?

949. How much interpersonal friction is there in your team?

950. How do you manage human resources?

951. To what degree do the goals specify concrete team work products?

952. Does more radicalness mean more perceived benefits?

953. To what degree do team members feel that the purpose of the team is important, if not exciting?

954. To what degree does the teams work approach provide opportunity for members to engage in open interaction?

955. To what degree is the team cognizant of small wins to be celebrated along the way?

956. To what degree is there a sense that only the team can succeed?

957. When a reviewer complains about method variance, what is the essence of the complaint?

958. To what degree are sub-teams possible or necessary?

959. Do friends perform better than acquaintances?

960. To what degree does the team possess adequate membership to achieve its ends?

961. What are you doing specifically to develop the leaders around you?

962. To what degree are the relative importance and priority of the goals clear to all team members?

963. To what degree do members articulate the goals beyond the team membership?

964. To what degree do all members feel responsible for all agreed-upon measures?

965. Lack of method variance in self-reported affect and perceptions at work: Reality or artifact?

3.9 Team Member Performance Assessment: Marketing Strategy And Execution

966. What is a significant fact or event?

967. To what degree do team members understand one anothers roles and skills?

968. Does adaptive training work?

969. What stakeholders must be involved in the development and oversight of the performance plan?

970. How do you create a self-sustaining capacity for a collaborative culture?

971. How do you currently use the time that is available?

972. What are the evaluation strategies (e.g., reaction, learning, behavior, results) used. What evaluation results did you have?

973. To what degree are the skill areas critical to team performance present?

974. Does the rater (supervisor) have to wait for the interim or final performance assessment review to tell an employee that the employees performance is unsatisfactory?

975. Who is responsible?

976. What changes do you need to make to align practices with beliefs?

977. What steps have you taken to improve performance?

978. What qualities does a successful Team leader possess?

979. How do you determine which data are the most important to use, analyze, or review?

980. What is a general description of the processes under performance measurement and assessment?

981. What happens if a team member receives a Rating of Unsatisfactory?

982. What evidence supports your decision-making?

983. What is the target group for instruction (e.g., individual and collective or small team instruction)?

984. What variables that affect team members achievement are within your control?

3.10 Issue Log: Marketing Strategy And Execution

985. How is this initiative related to other portfolios, programs, or Marketing Strategy And Execution projects?

986. Do you have members of your team responsible for certain stakeholders?

987. What effort will a change need?

988. Who were proponents/opponents?

989. Persistence; will users learn a work around or will they be bothered every time?

990. Is access to the Issue Log controlled?

991. Which stakeholders are thought leaders, influences, or early adopters?

992. Are the Marketing Strategy And Execution project issues uniquely identified, including to which product they refer?

993. What approaches to you feel are the best ones to use?

994. What is a Stakeholder?

995. Is the issue log kept in a safe place?

996. Are they needed?

997. What is a change?

998. Do you feel a register helps?

999. What would have to change?

1000. Is there an important stakeholder who is actively opposed and will not receive messages?

1001. How much time does it take to do it?

1002. How were past initiatives successful?

4.0 Monitoring and Controlling Process Group: Marketing Strategy And Execution

1003. How do you monitor progress?

1004. What do they need to know about the Marketing Strategy And Execution project?

1005. Were sponsors and decision makers available when needed outside regularly scheduled meetings?

1006. Feasibility: how much money, time, and effort can you put into this?

1007. Accuracy: what design will lead to accurate information?

1008. How is agile Marketing Strategy And Execution project management done?

1009. What factors are contributing to progress or delay in the achievement of products and results?

1010. Is there undesirable impact on staff or resources?

1011. Change, where should you look for problems?

1012. Overall, how does the program function to serve the clients?

1013. If action is called for, what form should it take?

1014. In what way has the program come up with innovative measures for problem-solving?

1015. Did you implement the program as designed?

1016. When will the Marketing Strategy And Execution project be done?

1017. User: who wants the information and what are they interested in?

1018. Did the Marketing Strategy And Execution project team have enough people to execute the Marketing Strategy And Execution project plan?

1019. If a risk event occurs, what will you do?

4.1 Project Performance Report: Marketing Strategy And Execution

1020. To what degree does the funding match the requirement?

1021. To what degree are the demands of the task compatible with and converge with the relationships of the informal organization?

1022. What is the degree to which rules govern information exchange between groups?

1023. What is in it for you?

1024. To what degree are the goals realistic?

1025. To what degree is there centralized control of information sharing?

1026. To what degree are the teams goals and objectives clear, simple, and measurable?

1027. To what degree does the informal organization make use of individual resources and meet individual needs?

1028. To what degree does the teams work approach provide opportunity for members to engage in results-based evaluation?

1029. To what degree will each member have the opportunity to advance his or her professional skills in all three of the above categories while contributing to the accomplishment of the teams purpose and goals?

1030. Next Steps?

1031. To what degree are the members clear on what they are individually responsible for and what they are jointly responsible for?

1032. To what degree are the tasks requirements reflected in the flow and storage of information?

1033. What is the degree to which rules govern information exchange between individuals within your organization?

1034. To what degree does the formal organization make use of individual resources and meet individual needs?

1035. To what degree can team members frequently and easily communicate with one another?

1036. To what degree are the goals ambitious?

4.2 Variance Analysis: Marketing Strategy And Execution

1037. Are the bases and rates for allocating costs from each indirect pool consistently applied?

1038. Can the relationship with problem customers be restructured so that there is a win-win situation?

1039. How are variances affected by multiple material and labor categories?

1040. Is all contract work included in the CWBS?

1041. Are overhead cost budgets established for each department which has authority to incur overhead costs?

1042. Did an existing competitor change strategy?

1043. How does your organization measure performance?

1044. Is the entire contract planned in time-phased control accounts to the extent practicable?

1045. What is the actual cost of work performed?

1046. Are data elements reconcilable between internal summary reports and reports forwarded to the stakeholders?

1047. Is the market likely to continue to grow at this

rate next year?

1048. What is the total budget for the Marketing Strategy And Execution project (including estimates for authorized and unpriced work)?

1049. How are material, labor, and overhead standards set?

1050. Are indirect costs accumulated for comparison with the corresponding budgets?

1051. Is data disseminated to the contractors management timely, accurate, and usable?

1052. How do you identify and isolate causes of favorable and unfavorable cost and schedule variances?

1053. Are there knowledgeable Marketing Strategy And Execution projections of future performance?

1054. Are significant decision points, constraints, and interfaces identified as key milestones?

1055. Are authorized changes being incorporated in a timely manner?

1056. Are the wbs and organizational levels for application of the Marketing Strategy And Execution projected overhead costs identified?

4.3 Earned Value Status: Marketing Strategy And Execution

1057. If earned value management (EVM) is so good in determining the true status of a Marketing Strategy And Execution project and Marketing Strategy And Execution project its completion, why is it that hardly any one uses it in information systems related Marketing Strategy And Execution projects?

1058. Earned value can be used in almost any Marketing Strategy And Execution project situation and in almost any Marketing Strategy And Execution project environment. it may be used on large Marketing Strategy And Execution projects, medium sized Marketing Strategy And Execution projects, tiny Marketing Strategy And Execution projects (in cut-down form), complex and simple Marketing Strategy And Execution projects and in any market sector. some people, of course, know all about earned value, they have used it for years - but perhaps not as effectively as they could have?

1059. How does this compare with other Marketing Strategy And Execution projects?

1060. How much is it going to cost by the finish?

1061. What is the unit of forecast value?

1062. Where is evidence-based earned value in your organization reported?

1063. Verification is a process of ensuring that the developed system satisfies the stakeholders agreements and specifications; Are you building the product right? What do you verify?

1064. Are you hitting your Marketing Strategy And Execution projects targets?

1065. Validation is a process of ensuring that the developed system will actually achieve the stakeholders desired outcomes; Are you building the right product? What do you validate?

1066. Where are your problem areas?

1067. When is it going to finish?

4.4 Risk Audit: Marketing Strategy And Execution

1068. Are you aware of the industry standards that apply to your operations?

1069. Do you have an understanding of insurance claims processes?

1070. Does your organization have a process for meeting its ongoing taxation obligations?

1071. What expertise do auditors need to generate effective business-level risk assessments, and to what extent do auditors currently possess the already stated attributes?

1072. Does your organization have an up-to-date constitution?

1073. Do you record and file all audits?

1074. How effective are your risk controls?

1075. Auditor independence: a burdensome constraint or a core value?

1076. Is the number of people on the Marketing Strategy And Execution project team adequate to do the job?

1077. Have reasonable steps been taken to reduce the risks to acceptable levels?

1078. Do industry specialists and business risk auditors enhance audit reporting accuracy?

1079. Are Marketing Strategy And Execution project requirements stable?

1080. Where will the next scandal or adverse media involving your organization come from?

1081. How do you compare to other jurisdictions when managing the risk of ....?

1082. Are you willing to seek legal advice when required?

1083. What effect would a better risk management program have had?

1084. What is the effect of globalisation; is business becoming too complex and can the auditor rely on auditing standards?

1085. Has everyone (staff, volunteers and participants) agreed to a code of behaviour or conduct?

4.5 Contractor Status Report: Marketing Strategy And Execution

1086. How is risk transferred?

1087. What are the minimum and optimal bandwidth requirements for the proposed solution?

1088. Describe how often regular updates are made to the proposed solution. Are corresponding regular updates included in the standard maintenance plan?

1089. What is the average response time for answering a support call?

1090. How long have you been using the services?

1091. Who can list a Marketing Strategy And Execution project as organization experience, your organization or a previous employee of your organization?

1092. If applicable; describe your standard schedule for new software version releases. Are new software version releases included in the standard maintenance plan?

1093. What was the actual budget or estimated cost for your organizations services?

1094. What was the overall budget or estimated cost?

1095. Are there contractual transfer concerns?

1096. What was the budget or estimated cost for your organizations services?

1097. How does the proposed individual meet each requirement?

1098. What process manages the contracts?

1099. What was the final actual cost?

4.6 Formal Acceptance: Marketing Strategy And Execution

1100. Was business value realized?

1101. General estimate of the costs and times to complete the Marketing Strategy And Execution project?

1102. Who supplies data?

1103. Was the Marketing Strategy And Execution project work done on time, within budget, and according to specification?

1104. How well did the team follow the methodology?

1105. Did the Marketing Strategy And Execution project manager and team act in a professional and ethical manner?

1106. What function(s) does it fill or meet?

1107. What are the requirements against which to test, Who will execute?

1108. What can you do better next time?

1109. Does it do what Marketing Strategy And Execution project team said it would?

1110. Did the Marketing Strategy And Execution project achieve its MOV?

1111. Was the Marketing Strategy And Execution project managed well?

1112. What was done right?

1113. What features, practices, and processes proved to be strengths or weaknesses?

1114. Was the Marketing Strategy And Execution project goal achieved?

1115. What lessons were learned about your Marketing Strategy And Execution project management methodology?

1116. What is the Acceptance Management Process?

1117. How does your team plan to obtain formal acceptance on your Marketing Strategy And Execution project?

1118. Have all comments been addressed?

1119. Who would use it?

5.0 Closing Process Group: Marketing Strategy And Execution

1120. Did the Marketing Strategy And Execution project team have the right skills?

1121. What will you do?

1122. What could be done to improve the process?

1123. Is this an updated Marketing Strategy And Execution project Proposal Document?

1124. What is the overall risk of the Marketing Strategy And Execution project to your organization?

1125. What is the Marketing Strategy And Execution project name and date of completion?

1126. Can the lesson learned be replicated?

1127. What were things that you need to improve?

1128. Did the Marketing Strategy And Execution project team have enough people to execute the Marketing Strategy And Execution project plan?

1129. Did you do things well?

1130. When will the Marketing Strategy And Execution project be done?

1131. How well did the chosen processes fit the needs

of the Marketing Strategy And Execution project?

1132. How will you know you did it?

1133. Will the Marketing Strategy And Execution project deliverable(s) replace a current asset or group of assets?

1134. What is the Marketing Strategy And Execution project Management Process?

1135. What business situation is being addressed?

1136. Just how important is your work to the overall success of the Marketing Strategy And Execution project?

1137. How will staff learn how to use the deliverables?

5.1 Procurement Audit: Marketing Strategy And Execution

1138. Are idle funds invested, and is interest distributed to the various activity accounts at least annually?

1139. Are review meetings organized during contract execution and do they meet demand?

1140. Does the approval include approval of prices?

1141. Did the contracting authority offer unrestricted and full electronic access to the contract documents and any supplementary documents (specifying the internet address in the notice)?

1142. Do appropriate controls ensure that procurement decisions are not biased by conflicts of interest or corruption?

1143. Were products/services not received within the prescribed time limit?

1144. Where your organization engaged an expert, was the contract awarded in compliance with procurement regulations?

1145. Are approval limits definitive as to amount and classification of expenditure?

1146. Is the procurement process organized the most appropriate way taking into consideration the amount of procurement?

1147. Has a deputy treasurer been appointed to sign checks when the treasurer is unable to perform that duty?

1148. Are checks used in numeric sequence?

1149. Are risks in the external environment identified, for example: Budgetary constraints?

1150. Are there established procedures for dealing with and documenting non-performance and return of goods?

1151. Is there no evidence that the expert has influenced the decisions taken by the public authority in his/her interest or in the interest of a specific contractor?

1152. Does your organization maintain a current file of vendors and vendor catalogues?

1153. Has the award included no items different from the already stated contained in bid specifications?

1154. Are transportation charges verified?

1155. Do at least two people have custodial responsibilities for negotiable checks (one checking on the other)?

1156. Are internal control mechanisms performed before payments?

1157. Are required quality and service standards set?

5.2 Contract Close-Out: Marketing Strategy And Execution

1158. Why Outsource?

1159. Was the contract sufficiently clear so as not to result in numerous disputes and misunderstandings?

1160. Parties: who is involved?

1161. Change in attitude or behavior?

1162. How/when used ?

1163. Change in knowledge?

1164. Parties: Authorized?

1165. Have all contracts been closed?

1166. Have all contracts been completed?

1167. Have all acceptance criteria been met prior to final payment to contractors?

1168. Has each contract been audited to verify acceptance and delivery?

1169. Have all contract records been included in the Marketing Strategy And Execution project archives?

1170. How does it work?

1171. What happens to the recipient of services?

1172. What is capture management?

1173. Are the signers the authorized officials?

1174. Was the contract type appropriate?

1175. How is the contracting office notified of the automatic contract close-out?

1176. Change in circumstances?

1177. Was the contract complete without requiring numerous changes and revisions?

5.3 Project or Phase Close-Out: Marketing Strategy And Execution

1178. Were risks identified and mitigated?

1179. What advantages do the an individual interview have over a group meeting, and vice-versa?

1180. Who is responsible for award close-out?

1181. What is the information level of detail required for each stakeholder?

1182. When and how were information needs best met?

1183. Planned remaining costs?

1184. What benefits or impacts does the stakeholder group expect to obtain as a result of the Marketing Strategy And Execution project?

1185. What process was planned for managing issues/risks?

1186. Who exerted influence that has positively affected or negatively impacted the Marketing Strategy And Execution project?

1187. Did the delivered product meet the specified requirements and goals of the Marketing Strategy And Execution project?

1188. What are the informational communication needs for each stakeholder?

1189. Was the user/client satisfied with the end product?

1190. Were cost budgets met?

1191. In preparing the Lessons Learned report, should it reflect a consensus viewpoint, or should the report reflect the different individual viewpoints?

1192. Were the outcomes different from the already stated planned?

1193. What was the preferred delivery mechanism?

1194. What are the marketing communication needs for each stakeholder?

1195. Did the Marketing Strategy And Execution project management methodology work?

5.4 Lessons Learned: Marketing Strategy And Execution

1196. What was the methodology behind successful learning experiences, and how might they be applied to the broader challenge of your organizations knowledge management?

1197. What are the internal dependencies?

1198. What are the influence patterns?

1199. How much communication is socially oriented?

1200. How useful do individuals find communications?

1201. What are the performance measures?

1202. What were the actual outcomes?

1203. How often do communications get lost?

1204. What were the main bottlenecks on the process?

1205. What could have been improved?

1206. How effective was the quality assurance process?

1207. Under what legal authority did your organization head and program manager direct your organization and Marketing Strategy And Execution project?

1208. What needs to be done over or differently?

1209. Who managed most of the communication within the Marketing Strategy And Execution project?

1210. For the next Marketing Strategy And Execution project, how could you improve on the way Marketing Strategy And Execution project was conducted?

1211. If you had to do this Marketing Strategy And Execution project again, what is the one thing that you would change (related to process, not to technical solutions)?

1212. What Marketing Strategy And Execution project circumstances were not anticipated?

1213. How effective was the documentation that you received with the Marketing Strategy And Execution project product/service?

Index

aspect 201
aspects   214-215
assess   23, 43, 87, 103, 130, 207, 210
assessed   88, 181, 206
assessing   98
Assessment   5-6, 9-10, 18, 197, 199, 206-207, 238, 240-241
assets   48, 259
assigned   33, 38, 142, 152, 156, 182, 214, 235
assigning   174
Assignment   5, 195
assist   9, 71, 95, 186
assistant   8
associated   232
assuming   203
Assumption   3, 154
assurance   23, 144, 198, 229, 266
attainable   36, 198
attained   203
attempted   36
attempting   96
attend 20, 236
attendance   41
attended   41
attention   12, 120
attitude   262
attitudes   224
attributes   4, 108, 165, 226, 252
audience   220
audited   262
auditing   17, 99, 120, 196, 253
auditor 252-253
auditors   252-253
audits   252
author 1
authority   63, 158, 197, 202-203, 248, 260-261, 266
authorized   143, 158, 196, 249, 262-263
automated   213
automatic   263
available   17, 24, 31, 34, 48, 67, 71, 85, 95, 125, 142, 160,
163-164, 166, 192, 203, 205, 207, 230, 240, 244
Average   12, 27, 44, 59, 76, 92, 105, 131, 177, 254
averse 208
avoiding   204

evolve 97
exactly 192, 198
examined   40
examining   232
example   2, 9, 13, 26, 74, 93, 155, 261
examples   8-9
exceed   157
exceeding   53
excellence   8, 30
excellent   56
except 159
excessive   204
exchange   246-247
exciting   238
exclude   86
execute   134, 245, 256, 258
executed   227
executing   6, 181, 189, 210, 221
Execution   1-7, 9-14, 16-59, 61-77, 79-105, 107-150, 152-159,
161-171, 173, 175, 177-189, 191, 193, 195-197, 199-205, 207-211,
213-215, 217-219, 221-229, 231, 234-236, 238, 240, 242, 244-246,
248-254, 256-260, 262, 264-267
executive   8, 113
executives   123
exercise   23
exerted   264
existence   207, 211
existing 10, 93, 110, 135-136, 146, 153, 248
expect 120, 178, 183, 264
expected   18, 36, 86, 118, 130, 187, 221, 230
experience   40, 114, 118, 129, 143, 167, 209, 254
experiment   115
expert 260-261
expertise   85, 252
experts 29
explained   10
explicit 233
explicitly   108
explore   68
exposures   88
expressed   133
extent 11, 21-23, 38, 140-141, 208, 248, 252
external   35, 48, 118, 199, 208-209, 232, 261

market 17, 168, 248, 250
marketer   8
Marketing   1-14, 16-59, 61-101, 103-105, 107-150, 152-159,
161-171, 173, 175, 177-189, 191, 193, 195-197, 199-205, 207-211,
213-215, 217-219, 221-229, 231, 234-236, 238, 240, 242, 244-246,
248-254, 256-260, 262, 264-267
markets   19, 138
material   158, 167, 191, 248-249
materials   1, 232
matrices   150
Matrix   3, 5, 138, 150, 195, 209, 222
matter 29, 46, 50
mature 146
maturing   208
Maximize   204
maximizing   107
maximum   134
meaning   165
meaningful   56, 109, 159, 204
measurable   32, 36, 135, 222, 246
measure   2, 10, 17, 20, 32, 37, 45, 48-51, 55-58, 61, 76-77,
80, 82, 86-87, 94, 96, 99, 104, 152, 185-187, 189, 191-192, 209, 248
measured   24, 46-47, 52, 54-55, 58, 88, 100, 212
measures   46, 50, 53-54, 58, 61, 65, 70, 73-74, 82, 99, 103-
104, 140, 189, 226, 239, 245, 266
measuring   96
mechanical   1
mechanics   225
mechanism   265
mechanisms   261
mechanized   213
medium   219, 250
meeting   29, 34, 103, 182, 187, 190, 198, 201, 223, 229, 231,
236-237, 252, 264
meetings   37, 40-41, 146, 152, 181, 199, 236, 244, 260
megatrends   117
member   6, 31, 116, 119, 173, 210, 223, 236, 240-241, 246
members   30, 37-38, 41, 95, 144-145, 153, 198, 201, 234, 236,
238-242, 246-247
membership   239
message   104, 219-220
messages   202, 237, 243
method   140, 142, 176, 191, 219, 239

project 2-4, 6-9, 24-25, 29, 48, 72-73, 75, 82, 98-100, 106, 108,
110, 114, 116-117, 121, 125-126, 128, 132-147, 149-150, 152-157,
159, 161-170, 173, 175, 177-189, 195-196, 199-200, 202-205, 207-
210, 213-214, 217-218, 221-224, 226-228, 234-235, 242, 244-246,
249-250, 252-254, 256-259, 262, 264-265, 267
projected   158, 195, 249
projects   2, 46, 112, 130, 132, 140, 150, 154, 156, 180, 183-
184, 201, 203, 207, 210, 223-224, 242, 250-251
promising   119
promote   56, 71
promptly   184
proper 96, 199
properly   29, 31
proponents   242
Proposal   215, 258
proposals   100, 222
proposed   16, 50, 55, 142-143, 149, 205, 216, 219, 254-255
protect   67, 121
protected   73
protection   107
proved 257
provide   19, 67, 118, 126, 128, 137, 141, 149, 158, 161, 177,
185, 196, 238, 246
provided   12, 97, 144, 175, 215
providers   88, 213
providing   96, 137, 153, 188, 232-233
provision   161
public 213, 261
published   215
publisher   1
pulled 130
purchase   8, 176
purpose   2, 10, 120, 174, 185, 193, 226, 229, 236, 238, 247
pushing   110
qualified   30, 61, 64, 67, 142, 181
qualifies   64, 69
qualify 74
qualities   20, 241
quality 1, 4, 6, 10, 23, 48-49, 61, 69, 84, 96, 103, 129, 141, 144,
161, 189-194, 197-199, 207, 213, 218, 226, 229, 231-232, 261, 266
quantified   95
question   11-12, 16, 28, 45, 60, 77, 93, 106, 121, 193
questions   8-9, 11, 75, 177, 202-203, 231-232

298

reports 99, 137, 143, 152, 196, 200, 248
repository   217
represent   88, 227-228
reproduced   1
reputation   115
request   6, 75, 147, 187, 200, 225, 227-228
requested   1, 86, 133, 228
requests   213, 225
require 28, 48, 71, 73, 93, 102, 135, 171
required   19, 26, 31, 35, 40, 42, 48, 59, 62, 66, 78, 82, 103,
133, 141, 147-148, 160, 163, 165-166, 176, 180, 194, 206-207, 209,
219, 253, 261, 264
requiring   137, 263
research   17, 119, 127, 168, 237
Reserve   184
reserved   1
reserves   158
reside 90, 216
resolution   67, 79
resolve 18-19, 21, 166, 234
resolved   180-181, 184
resource   4-5, 112, 140, 144, 158, 166, 171, 173, 181, 199-
200, 204, 224
resources   2, 8, 17, 24-25, 31, 34, 36, 56, 65, 78, 102-103, 108,
112, 121, 142, 144, 148, 160, 163, 165-166, 173, 177, 183, 186,
221, 238, 244, 246-247
respect   1
respond   196
responded   12
responding   205
response   17, 19, 96, 101-104, 254
responses   85, 117, 215
responsive   185
result   67, 78, 88, 153, 185, 228, 262, 264
resultant   215
resulted   95
resulting   65, 140, 158
results 9, 36, 43, 50, 75, 77, 79, 84, 86-88, 91, 97, 99, 133, 144,
165, 176, 184, 186, 189, 191-192, 194, 240, 244
Retain 106
retained   64
retention   49
retrospect   130

second 12
section 12, 27, 44, 59, 76, 92, 104-105, 130-131
sector 250
securing 53, 126
security 17, 83, 101, 103, 137, 154, 190, 227, 231
segmented 39
segments 29, 122
select 63, 94
selected 91, 185-186
selecting 63, 126
Selection 5, 215-216, 222, 238
seller 175
sellers 1
selling 110, 229
senior 99, 108, 116
sensitive 53
sequence 163, 170, 261
sequencing 110, 140, 176
series 11
service 1-2, 8, 80, 84, 88, 103, 119, 153, 168, 206, 223, 261, 267
services 1, 28, 49, 55-56, 121, 124, 126, 139, 205, 222, 231-232, 236, 254-255, 260, 263
session 179
setbacks 61, 70
setting 108, 123
several 71
severely 66
shared 102, 186
sharing 101, 236, 246
shifts 20
short-term 204
should 8, 17-18, 20, 24, 30, 35-36, 41, 47-48, 62-64, 68-70, 81, 87, 89, 100, 104, 113-114, 117, 119, 126, 133-135, 137, 141, 146, 152, 159, 173, 198, 203, 205-206, 208-210, 215-216, 220-221, 227, 234-235, 244, 265
signature 112
signatures 171
signers 263
similar 29, 36, 72, 75, 165, 169, 207
simple 114, 196, 246, 250
simply 9, 229
single 129
single-use 8

supervisor   240
supplier   83, 127
suppliers   28, 70, 73
supplies   256
supply 59, 167
support   8, 17, 72, 94-95, 100, 108, 126, 128, 135, 149, 171, 197, 206, 213, 230-231, 254
supported   61
supporting   82, 96, 194
supportive   197
supports   241
supposed   196
surface   103
SUSTAIN   2, 89, 106
sustained   184
sustaining   98, 237
symptom   16, 59
system 10, 40, 63, 75, 95, 114, 136, 146, 148-149, 155, 158, 196, 199, 227, 230-232, 251
systematic   51, 57
systems   51, 61, 66, 73-74, 87, 96, 154, 159, 219, 222, 231-232, 250
tackle 59
tactics 229-230
takers 152
taking 46, 224, 260
talent 64, 116
talents 108
talking 8
tangle 196
target 42, 109, 241
targets 123, 222, 251
tasked 99
taxation   252
technical   85, 148, 267
techniques   67, 115, 133
technology   47, 81, 103, 119, 138, 148, 168, 208-209, 236-237
template   179
templates   8-9
testable   38
test-cycle   193
tested 21, 190
testing 208

CPSIA information can be obtained
at www.ICGtesting.com
Printed in the USA
BVHW041009200819
556236BV00011B/637/P